UCLan
3 0 APR 2015
LEARNING & INFORMATION
SERVICE

CREATING LANGUAGE CRIMES

CREATING LANGUAGE CRIMES

How Law Enforcement Uses (and Misuses) Language

ROGER W. SHUY

2005

OXFORD
UNIVERSITY PRESS

Oxford University Press, Inc., publishes works that further
Oxford University's objective of excellence
in research, scholarship, and education.

Oxford   New York
Auckland   Cape Town   Dar es Salaam   Hong Kong   Karachi
Kuala Lumpur   Madrid   Melbourne   Mexico City   Nairobi
New Delhi   Shanghai   Taipei   Toronto

With offices in
Argentina   Austria   Brazil   Chile   Czech Republic   France   Greece
Guatemala   Hungary   Italy   Japan   Poland   Portugal   Singapore
South Korea   Switzerland   Thailand   Turkey   Ukraine   Vietnam

Copyright © 2005 by Oxford University Press, Inc.

Published by Oxford University Press, Inc.
198 Madison Avenue, New York, New York 10016

www.oup.com

Oxford is a registered trademark of Oxford University Press

All rights reserved. No part of this publication may be reproduced,
stored in a retrieval system, or transmitted, in any form or by any means,
electronic, mechanical, photocopying, recording, or otherwise,
without the prior permission of Oxford University Press.

Library of Congress Cataloging-in-Publication Data
Shuy, Roger W.
Creating language crimes : how law enforcement uses (and misuses) language /
Roger W. Shuy.
p. cm.
Includes bibliographical references and index.
ISBN-13 978-0-19-518166-1
ISBN 0-19-518166-2
1. Undercover operations—United States.   2. Police—United States—
Language.   3. Communication in law enforcement—United States.
4. Forensic linguistics—United States.   I. Title.
HV8080.U5S38 2005
363.2'01'4—dc22   2004061709

1 3 5 7 9 8 6 4 2

Printed in the United States of America
on acid-free paper

PREFACE

Linguistics has been a wonderful life-framework for me. I can think of no field of study that is broader or has more relationships with the rest of human existence, since language is involved in virtually all of human activity. It is the primary and essential medium for conducting business, health, education, diplomacy, philosophy, politics, religion, and, as I show in this book, law. It is also important in areas where its influence is less suspected, such as art, music, and even in mathematics and the hard sciences. Sir Francis Bacon once claimed that all knowledge should be our province. The field of linguistics, with its broad-ranging potential, surely must come close to this. Many of the ideas found in this book come from my thirty-year association with Georgetown University, especially with my good friends and linguistic colleagues there, Deborah Tannen, Ralph Fasold, Deborah Schiffrin, and Heidi Hamilton. They, of course, are not to be held responsible for any of my misunderstandings or misstatements of their work here.

This book grows out of my twenty-five years of working with attorneys on criminal and civil cases. I stumbled into the application of linguistics to the legal setting quite by accident, while chatting with a lawyer sitting next to me on a flight from Washington, D.C., to Dallas early in 1979. Since that time I've consulted on some five hundred cases and testified at trial in a little over a tenth of them. I owe what little I know about the legal process from most of the lawyers I've worked with, just as I've learned about linguistics from those who nurtured me and from colleagues whose work continues to update me. I dedicate this book to those attorneys whose cases I describe here, along with my many forensic linguist friends who are devoted to making linguistics more accessible and useful to the legal profession. For their sage advice and for bearing with me and encouraging me all these years, I am also deeply indebted to my wife, best friend, and colleague, Jana Staton, and to my three wonderful children, Timothy Shuy, Joel Shuy, and Katie Shuy.

CONTENTS

Introduction ix

Part I: Language Crimes, Conversational Strategies, and Language Power

1. How Language Crimes Are Created 3
2. Conversational Strategies Used to Create Crimes 13
3. The Power of Conversational Strategies 31

Part II: Uses by Cooperating Witnesses

4. Overlapping, Ambiguity, and the Hit and Run in a Solicitation to Murder Case: *Texas v. T. Cullen Davis* 41

5. Retelling, Scripting, and Lying in a Murder Case: *Florida v. Alan Mackerley* 51

6. Interrupting, Overlapping, Lying, Not Taking "No" for an Answer, and Representing Illegality Differently to Separate Targets in a Stolen Property Case: *US v. Prakesh Patel and Daniel Houston* 59

7. Eleven Little Ambiguities and How They Grew in a Business Fraud Case: *US v. Paul Webster and Joe Martino* 69

8. Discourse Ambiguity in a Contract Fraud Case:
   US v. David Smith   81

9. Contamination and Manipulation in a Bribery Case:
   US v. Paul Manziel   89

10. Scripting by Requesting Directives and Apologies in a Sexual Misconduct Case: *Idaho v. J. Mussina*   99

Part III: Uses by Law Enforcement Officers

11. Police Camouflaging in an Obstruction of Justice Case:
    US v. Brian Lett   109

12. Police Camouflaging in a Purchasing Stolen Property Case: *US v. Tariq Shalash*   117

13. A Rogue Cop and Every Strategy He Can Think Of:
    The Wenatchee Washington Sex Ring Case   129

14. An Undercover Policeman Uses Ambiguity, Hit and Run, Interrupting, Scripting, and Refusing to Take "No" for an Answer in a Solicitation to Murder Case:
    The Crown v. Mohammed Arshad   137

15. Manipulating the Tape, Interrupting, Inaccurate Restatements, and Scripting in a Murder Case:
    Florida v. Jerry Townsend   159

Part IV: Conversational Strategies as Evidence

16. Eight Questions about the Power of Conversational Strategies in Undercover Police Investigations   167

References Cited   187

Cases Cited   190

Index   191

INTRODUCTION

Things are not always what they seem. We all know how people can give the impression that they have done something that they really haven't done, or haven't even considered doing. In much of life the ability to make a good impression can be very useful. It may help us get a good job, a good mate, a good grade in school, or even help us get elected to a political office. There is a fine line, perhaps, between giving a somewhat better impression than we deserve and being deceptive or outright lying. Yet we have become accustomed to such practice from the many advertisements and promotions that we see in the media. Self-puffery seems to be an integral part of our daily lives. But whatever the good side this practice may hold, it also has its downside, especially when the impression we try to make eventually bites us and yields an effect that is opposite of the one we intended. At such times we can (and should) be called to account for being misleading or giving a false impression.

Unfortunately, there are also ways that some people can use language to create the impression that our words mean something that we really didn't intend. If we are attentive and alert enough, we might be able to notice this, object to it, and try to repair it. But if we don't see it coming, we don't even notice it, and we let it pass unchallenged, this newly created false understanding can hurt us badly. Such things go by quickly in everyday conversation. When tape recordings of our conversations are played back at a later time and to other people, when we are not even there to defend ourselves, another serious complication follows.

When the act of creating a misleading impression is limited to the more mundane activities of life, we can usually steel ourselves to it and muddle along somehow. But when giving such misleading impressions causes targets or suspects in criminal cases to appear to have said something or agreed to something that they have not, the misleading impression can turn into a very serious matter—the loss of one's freedom—or even worse.

I make no claim that all, or even many, undercover operations carried out by law enforcement agencies regularly engage in the practice of creating false illusions about their targets' guilt. However, in the quarter century that I have been analyzing tape-recorded sting operations and police interrogations, I have seen an ample number of instances that qualify as the kind of linguistic unfairness that can land people in prison when they only thought they had said something noninculpatory and benign. Sometimes a clearly guilty person is tricked this way, and he or she clearly deserves to go to prison anyway. But even then, this does not excuse this practice. Law claims to be about the weight of evidence, not about impressions, or illusions, or mere suggestions of guilt. As O. J. Simpson's lawyer, Johnnie Cochran, once put it to the jury, "If the glove doesn't fit, you must acquit."

In fairness, we must understand that professions such as law enforcement see things with what Goodwin (1996) calls their own professional vision, an organized way of seeing and understanding events. Goodwin cites three criteria that create the vision of a profession: (1) coding, which transforms phenomena into the objects of knowledge that animate the discourse; (2) highlighting, which makes specific phenomena salient; and (3) producing and articulating a material representation. In short, the vision given us by our profession tends to make us see things through its own lenses. Linguists, for example, have their own lens of seeing language, one that is quite different from that of nonlinguists. The profession of law enforcement does much the same thing with its own lens. Goodwin describes how professional vision operates: "The sequence of talk...provides a relevant language game that can be used to make inferences about precisely which features of the complex perceptual field being pointed at should be attended to"(255).

Goodwin illustrates the professional vision of law enforcement with a brief story about a man who was brutally beaten by a policeman. The professional vision of law enforcement caused the police to see signs of the man's aggression that justified beating him. Their professional vision caused them to see the assault through a different lens, which turned things around to make it appear that the man had acted aggressively. The professional vision of the police coded aggression, highlighted it in their coding system, then articulated it in the language used to justify their attack on the man. Everyone makes use of their own professional vision in everyday life, but we should be alert to the fact that it can also interfere with finding truth. It is one thing for law enforcement to have this professional vision but quite another not to be able to realize when it may get in the way of understanding what is actually happening.

This book is about language evidence, not the more commonly known physical evidence such as DNA, fingerprints, or hair and fiber analysis. Its major focus is on the language used in undercover operations, when cooperating witnesses and policemen wear hidden microphones and covertly tape-record their targets. The cases in which I describe such evidence range widely from charges of murder, solicitation to murder, purchasing stolen property, business fraud, bribery, and obstruction of justice. The targets are millionaires, average people, business tycoons, salesmen, and even lawyers. All find themselves in criminal cases that show how unfair conversational strategies can be used on virtually anyone and at any time.

This book describes one aspect of forensic linguistics, part of the growing body of forensic science of our time. Most of the time, the techniques used by forensic scientists enable the legal process to ferret out the innocent from the guilty. But it doesn't always work that well. For example, in recent years considerable attention has been given to the way evidence can be tainted by forensic scientists. In 1994 *USA Today* and the Gannett News Service published the results of their survey of the past twenty years, which found eighty-five instances where prosecutors knowingly or unknowingly used tainted forensic evidence to convict the innocent or free the guilty (Larra Frank and John Hanchette, "Convicted on False Evidence?: False Science Often Sways Juries, Judges," July 19, 1994). The more notorious examples of police forensic laboratories include the fifteen years of forensic work of Fred Zain in West Virginia and Texas, who testified about evidence that he had never even analyzed and subsequently was accused of falsification and fraud in many other cases. The less than scientific work of some forensic pathologists, dentists, anthropologists, seriologists, and police laboratories is summarized by Kelly and Wearne (1998).

There are multiple reasons why forensic science has been misused, including the lack of an accreditation program that would ensure consistent uses of the valuable tools offered by science. For example, in 1995 Collaborative Testing Services tried to determine the extent to which fingerprint examiners were proficient and consistent in their findings. Of the 156 U.S. fingerprint examiners tested on seven latent prints, only 44 percent identified all seven correctly while 56 percent got at least one wrong, and 4 percent failed to identify any of the seven. Obviously, fingerprint analysis could do with some standard accreditation procedures.

An equally important problem with the current use of forensic science is an overwhelming desire by some law enforcement personnel to capture the bad guys despite the presence of actual evidence that might exonerate them. In cases that make use of hard data such as fingerprints or laboratory equipment, this can lead to cutting corners or even falsifying the data. In the case of tape-recorded language data, it can lead those wearing the undercover microphone to resort to using language strategies that can make the target look guilty. Nor is such tainting of evidence limited to undercover investigators. It can happen in police interrogations and in the courtroom as well, perhaps with less frequency.

Scientific equipment such as microscopes, infrared spectroscopes, computers, X-ray spectrometry, neutron activation, statistics, and, of course, DNA, have become hot topics in forensic science. But often overlooked are some of the more obvious uses of science, including linguistics. Most people use language so easily and naturally that they tend to not really see it very well. What people hear is often colored by their own professional vision, schemas, presuppositions, and expectations. If they believe that their targets are guilty, they tend to take the targets' words as an indication of guilt even when these words are not so intended. In criminal cases where the language is used as the evidence, it is imperative that such language be addressed with the same scientific objectivity, rigor, and accuracy that we expect of any other kind of forensic evidence. If it is tainted by the way the representative of law enforcement asks questions or otherwise distorts reality, the courts are bound to recognize it by following the scientific requirements of objectivity, factuality, and reasonable scientific certainty. Since most people, including law enforcement officers, lawyers, and judges, are not linguistically trained, they can be blinded by what appears to them to be guilt-producing evidence when, in actuality, they may have little or no foundation upon which to base their perceptions. This book is an effort to illuminate one area of forensic linguistics that should be understood and considered in certain types of criminal cases—the way conversational strategies can lead to indictments and affect the outcome of trials.

I am not suggesting that there is a recent epidemic of undercover language unfairness stalking the land. Chances are that the phenomenon has been relatively stable, at least since tape-recorded evidence has been made available for analysis. The temptation to cut corners and get an "obviously" guilty person convicted is sometimes difficult to overcome, especially for cooperating witnesses, who have their own personal reasons for doing what they do. Although in chapters 4 through 10, cooperating witnesses wear the mike and do the linguistic damage, their supervising law enforcement officers are by no means excusable. They are either duped by the clever turns of phrase used by their operatives or they become witting or unwitting victims of their own professional vision in which such false impressions are created. In fact, law enforcement officers often do the same things. To illustrate this point, this book includes six chapters that show how law enforcement officers used most of the same conversational strategies that cooperating witnesses used to make their targets look guilty. Two of these six chapters involve an undercover cop who camouflages the criminality of what he proposes to the target (chapters 11 and 12). Another chapter describes what can only be called a rogue cop who used every linguistic trick he could think of to get a number of people indicted in a huge sex scandal (chapter 13). Still another chapter shows how a Scottish undercover officer uses five conversational strategies to make it appear that his target is soliciting murder (chapter 14). The most outrageous of all, however, is the way detectives manipulate the tape recording, script the mentally retarded suspect, and constantly interrupt him (chapter 15). For those further interested in how language can be misused by police interrogators and prosecutors, I suggest reading my earlier books, *Language Crimes* (1993) and *The Language of Confession, Interrogation and Deception* (1998). For readers interested in specific types of crimes, the following index may be helpful:

> murder: chapters 5 and 15
> solicitation to murder: chapters 4 and 14
> purchasing stolen property: chapters 6 and 12
> business fraud: chapters 7 and 8
> sexual misconduct: chapters 10 and 13
> bribery: chapter 9
> obstruction of justice: chapter 11

Since the major intention of this book is only to show how powerful conversational strategies are used by law enforcement in undercover operations, the cases are not described in depth. The judicial outcomes are not relevant when the power of conversational strategies is the focus. Who wins or loses is immaterial. The ways these eleven conversational strategies were employed is my central focus.

The intended readers of this book are primarily forensic linguists, discourse analysts, criminologists, defense attorneys, prosecutors, and judges. If the general public also finds the book interesting, I will be delighted.

PART I

Language Crimes, Conversational Strategies, and Language Power

How language crimes are created, a description of eleven conversational strategies, and the way these strategies evidence power.

1

How Language Crimes Are Created

Often, if not usually, law enforcement has good reason to suspect that a target is up to no good. Until the police began to take advantage of recording devices, investigating crime in which the language used, what I call language crimes, was very difficult, often depending on the questionable memories and words of witnesses. In suspected white-collar, solicitation, and bribery/extortion cases, where actual language is the best evidence, undercover tape recordings are now made of conversations with the targets. In most, but not all, jurisdictions, tape recordings are also made of police interrogations with suspects. Unfortunately, it is rare that a tape recording is made of the trial itself, which is normally preserved only through the written transcript prepared by a court reporter. Tape recordings guarantee the accuracy and verifiability of the actual words being used, eliminating the need to depend on the veracity of an accuser, a witness, or even a court reporter.

All three sources of electronically recorded language evidence are susceptible to linguistic analysis. The most preferable is videotaped evidence, since it includes important clues about nonverbal communication, distances the speakers and listeners are from each other, and, in fact, whether or not the target was even present when crucial information is put on tape. Audiotapes do not capture these linguistic clues but they are preferable to written transcripts, which do not capture voice intonation, pause length, and other orally transmitted indications of meaning.

There are three contexts in which linguistic analysis of what was actually said can be helpful: the data gathering process, the interrogation by police, and the trial itself. In each of these it is possible for the undercover agent, the police interrogator, and the prosecutor to create an illusion that a suspect has committed a crime, which, when analyzed linguistically, may be shown to be not supportable.

1. During undercover tape-recording of suspects, sometimes agents or cooperating witnesses use language strategies that offer the illusion that the target is currently involved in committing a crime or has committed a criminal act in the past.
2. During the police interrogation, some suspects may eventually break down and admit to crimes that they never actually committed. This is generally referred to as the false confession (Leo and Ofshe 1997; Ofshe and Leo 1998). The way questions are asked and answered can also reveal language strategies that are subject to linguistic analysis.
3. During the trial, prosecutors also may use language strategies that can make it appear that defendants are guilty of crimes that they never committed (Shuy 1998).

These three contexts for law enforcement and the prosecution to create the illusion that a crime has been committed should be distinguished from an acceptable form of deception by the government—that of inventing an entire false identification in a sting operation. For example, in the midst of suspected telecommunication fraud, the government might set up a fake company and use its undercover agents as employees or representatives of that fictitious business in order either to obtain from targets a confession of past illegal acts or to tempt potential offenders to engage in ongoing or future unlawful activities. This act of creating a criminal scenario is a generally acceptable law enforcement technique but it is not the subject of this book.

Here we are concerned with the category of creating crimes that is not always apparent to the average person, including law enforcement officers and prosecutors. Until recently, considerable analysis has been made of the police interrogation and the courtroom language used by prosecutors. But, as far as I can see, very little work has focused on the way undercover operatives in a sting case can bend and twist conversations to suit the goals of an eventual prosecution.

It should be clear that I am not saying that all suspects are guiltless about something; only that the specific evidence gathered against them sometimes bears considerable scrutiny that can offer reason to believe that the persons wearing the mike or asking the questions are manipulating the conversation, consciously or unconsciously, to make the suspects look guilty. This phenomenon has gone relatively unanalyzed, perhaps because it virtually always consists of audio- or videotape recorded language data that appear to be more troublesome for the legal process to handle. It also involves linguistic understandings of how language actually works.

The field of law is usually more comfortable dealing with the written word. Written trial transcripts can be reviewed for that particular kind of representation, absent the necessary omissions of the visual clues offered by videotape and the auditory signals of meaning offered by audiotape that might more clearly describe the way language is used in the courtroom. To complicate matters further, even when police interrogations are taped, they frequently do not include the entire interviewing process, often leaving out the conversation that led up to the eventual confession. Even in undercover operations, sometimes only parts of the conversations are tape-recorded, as will be shown in some of the chapters in this book.

How can such manipulation of language evidence, whether intentional or unintentional, ever happen? First of all, the persons wearing the undercover mike, directing the police interrogation and questioning witnesses at trial begin their work with a distinct power advantage over those they talk with. They know the significance, even the minute connotations, of what is being asked and answered. In undercover conversations, when the targets think they are simply engaged in an everyday conversation, they are less on alert and are frequently less careful about how they say things. The persons doing the taping, in contrast, have the power to decide when to tape, who to tape, when to start the taping, when to stop, and even how to slant the conversation to serve their own ends. They also have the power to tape-record when the targets are not even present, when the targets are not listening, when they are preoccupied with something else, or when they are well out of hearing range.

In the interrogation room and in the courtroom, targets may be more alert to the importance of what they say since the social relationship between participants is knowingly unequal, offering more power to the ones whose status in the social relationship is superordinate, or higher. Examples of this in everyday life include the status of a teacher over a student, a physician over a patient, a boss over an employee, or a person buying a product over the person trying to sell it. Such relationships assign innate power to the superordinate over the subordinate. Evidence of such power is often revealed by features of the language used, such as who talks the most, who introduces the most topics, who asks the questions, and who makes the ultimate decisions about times and places of meetings.

The subordinate participants are required to be polite, if not passive, when a course grade is to be challenged, when an illness is to be healed, when a report is to be accepted, when a sale is to be made, and when they are accused of a crime. In short, the subordinate persons are required to give leeway, to not disagree violently, to suppress discomfort, to wait for the idea to be played out before renegotiating, and to hold their emotions in check.

As the following chapters point out, the superordinate persons can use conversation strategies that are not available to the subordinate ones. They can interrupt without complaint or censure, they can change the subject, they can be as ambiguous as they want, and they can decide on how to use their words and react to the words of the targets as they see fit.

In my earlier book, *Language Crimes* (1993), I described the sort of crime that is accomplished through language alone. Physical crimes involve assault, robbery, murder, or other forms of human injury. But there are other types of criminal activity that are accomplished only through talk. I call these language crimes. This category includes the physically nonviolent crimes of bribery, solicitation to murder, sex solicitation, business fraud, selling or purchasing stolen property, perjury, threatening, and other offenses. The language used may be written or spoken. When it is written, the evidence resides in documents of various types. When it is spoken, the evidence is usually in the form of audio- or videotape recordings.

On the surface it would seem that such written or spoken evidence of a language crime would be adequate to convict the target, but this is not always the case. Sometimes the prosecution interprets ambiguous understandings about what is said in ways favorable only to its own case, as in *United States v. John Z. DeLorean* (Shuy 1993). When this happens, careful analysis of such ambiguity can help the defendant by showing that more than one meaning is possible. In cases of alleged bribery it is necessary for the prosecution to show that an actual bribe was either offered or accepted from the language found on the tape. This is another language event that linguists, using speech act analysis, can help clarify. There are standards of what constitutes a felicitous offer and a felicitous agreement. If such standards are not met, the evidence may not show what the prosecution claims it shows (Shuy 1993). Even when the police elicit what appears to be a confession from the target, linguistic analysis of the actual questions and answers can lead to interpretations quite different from those that the investigators believe (Shuy 1998).

Of course when the language evidence against targets is clear and unambiguous, they have little chance of a successful defense. Things are as they should be. The guilty are convicted and go to prison. If the world were always this clear and simple, there would be no need for this book. However, it has been clearly shown that the innocent are sometimes convicted of crimes that they didn't actually commit (Scheck, Neufeld, and Dwyer 2000). Since there is no full equivalent to incontrovertible DNA evidence in most language crimes, there is a need for a careful analysis of the language used by law enforcement and by targets when their conversations are surreptitiously tape-recorded, as well as when they are interrogated by undercover police officers and by prosecutors.

Ideally in undercover operations, agents or cooperating witnesses plan their undercover conversations with targets using the following four steps.

1. First, let the targets do the talking in the hope that they will self-generate their own guilt, that they will say something incriminating without being prodded into it. This is the best kind of evidence, since there can be no question about whether or not it was unduly influenced by law enforcement. But things don't always go quite that smoothly, pointing to the need for step two.

2. If self-generated guilt doesn't occur, the next step for the person wearing the mike is to drop hints of illegality, hoping that the targets will catch them and perhaps develop them further, thereby implicating themselves in the crime. This works well if the targets are inclined toward such criminality in the first place, but it can flop ingloriously when the targets either don't catch the hint or aren't criminally disposed in the first place. If such is the case, the need is to go to step three.
3. A third step is to get the targets to retell an incident from the past that the agent or cooperating witness pretends to not remember completely or accurately (the retell strategy). If the targets have indeed done something incriminating in the past and if they retell this event accurately on tape, they are caught and the evidence is damning. If they don't retell the event in the way that the agent or cooperating witness hopes, it may be because the targets' interpretation of this alleged past criminal act was not criminal at all. Naturally, it also may be the case that they simply refuse to retell an event for which they really were guilty of doing something illegal. If this step fails, there is always step four.
4. When hinting and retelling fail to bring out the targets' guilt, the fourth step is for the agent or cooperating witness to become flat-out clear and unambiguous about the nature of the crime that is hinted at, discussed, or proposed. This provides the targets the opportunity to clearly and unambiguously agree or disagree. If they agree to become involved in the criminal activity, the targets are successfully caught on tape. If they disagree, the operation probably should be over and law enforcement should look elsewhere for the perpetrator. Even then it's sometimes hard for law enforcement to give up.

Sometimes it's even hard for law enforcement officers to apply step four, since it requires them to be explicit and unambiguous. One of the FBI Guidelines for undercover operations is that the agent or cooperating witness must represent the nature of the activity clearly and unambiguously. Oddly enough, this guideline seems to be not very well known among law enforcement officers. When I pointed this guideline out in a workshop that I once gave for Drug Enforcement Administration (DEA) agents, their reactions were close to shock and disbelief. More than one agent told me, "If I'm clear to the target that what I'm proposing is illegal, he'll walk away." There are probably two reasons why their target's response is accurate. One is that a guilty target might get suspicious of anyone who is being so unambiguous and clear and therefore choose to opt out of the deal. The other is that the target is innocent and would say "no" to such a deal once its illegality is made clear. I had a hard time convincing the agents of the second possibility. Their resistance must have been ingrained in their professional vision. Some undercover officers appear to fear losing a guilty target more than they fear entrapping an innocent one.

The agents' problem here is that too often they tend to rush too quickly in their undercover operations. The FBI Guideline does not specify that the agent must be clear and unambiguous about the proposed illegality from the outset of the conversation. The best evidence they can get is when the target self-generates his own guilt without prompting or influence (Sandoval 2003). This is what police interviewers are advised to do when they talk with suspects. Interview manuals are in agreement that at first it is better to let the suspect talk and talk, without interruption and without specific questions to guide them. The same is true for undercover operations. It will normally take longer this way but the evidence elicited can be much stronger. The four-step planned procedure noted above is more effective and efficient in the long run. If self-generated guilt doesn't happen, move next to hints and requests for retelling. If that doesn't work, there is nothing more to do than to follow the FBI Guideline—to express clearly and unambiguously the illegal nature of the criminal nature of the activity.

Somewhere in this four-step procedure the targets will either be caught by their own words or they will walk away from the agents' suggestions, perhaps because they are really innocent. But when the investigation appears to be failing to net the targets, some agents and cooperating witnesses simply won't give up. When this happens, they sometimes resort to other techniques or, as I call them in this book, conversational strategies.

This book shows how the appearance of a crime can be created in undercover sting operations and, although it is not the focus of this book, the same is true, perhaps to a lesser extent, when used by police interrogators and prosecutors. One major problem stems from the use of what the government calls "cooperating witnesses," those who wear a hidden mike and talk with the targets. Most government undercover agents are not skilled in complex things such as business fraud or in the underworld, where solicitation to murder is a more comfortable topic. The logical way for police to address this issue is to find someone who is skilled in such things and seems to fit the proper and believable profile. Many law enforcement agencies use cooperating witnesses as an answer to this problem.

Usually, cooperating witnesses have already been caught in the overall crime being investigated. Thus, persons caught in buying or selling stolen goods may be able to help law enforcement find others doing the same thing, or at least know about others doing the same thing. The police then wire them up and send them out to capture others who are willing to buy or sell stolen property.

Why would cooperating witnesses agree to do this? Simply because they are offered certain considerations at sentencing if they cooperate with the police in this way. And here begins the problem. It is obviously in the best interest of the cooperating witness to be successful, in this case to capture a language crime on tape. Often they are efficient con men themselves, and sometimes this approach works perfectly and honestly. But sometimes it doesn't. Cooperating witnesses stand to gain a lot if they help capture other targets. To accomplish this, they are not averse to using ambiguity and other strategies described in this book in order to make the tape they produce look as though their targets are actually committing a crime even if they are not. In other words, many cooperating witnesses have reason to try to create the illusion of a crime where none actually exists.

Another problem is more troublesome. The adversarial nature of the legal system is well known in Western law. Attorneys on both sides are obliged to do the best they can in order to win their cases. This system may be perfectly acceptable for the courts, but its place is questionable in the process of intelligence gathering. Intelligence is the objective gathering of evidence about a suspected problem. It is not judgmental. It is not biased for or against the target. The job is to simply gather the evidence. This evidence becomes the first step toward a conviction, but, in itself, it is not the conviction. When undercover operatives apply some or all of the strategies described in this book to make it appear that targets are guilty when they are not, the intelligence process is seriously compromised.

In fairness to law enforcement, it should be said that the use of unfair language strategies to produce the unjust appearance of guilt appears to be a bit more common among cooperating witnesses than among police or prosecutors. The occasional "rogue cop" is not commonplace. During trial, a competent defense attorney always has the opportunity to object to what may seem to be unfair questions by the prosecutor. But undercover operators have a much freer range and pose a much greater problem, not only to targets but also to the police who supervise the operation from a distance. With respect to the use of cooperating witnesses, if law enforcement is guilty of anything, it is that they sometimes don't monitor the taping very well or, worse yet, that their professional vision makes them so intent on capturing the target that they may fail to notice the language ambiguities and other evidence of the targets' noninvolvement. In doing so they also fail in the appropriate underlying intelligence process.

Much of the time we use language fairly unconsciously. We usually don't stop to consider how we pronounce our words or how we put our sentences together. We may struggle more consciously sometimes to find the exact word we want to convey but, on the whole, we talk without thinking about how we do it. After all, we've been speaking our language since early childhood. In the same way, we are not conscious of the laws of physics or optics when we ride a bicycle, drive a car, or climb the stairs. If we were to think about the mechanics of what we are doing, we would ruin the automaticity of the event and possibly cause an accident for ourselves. In contrast, the language strategies used to create the illusion of criminality seem to be frequently carried out deliberately.

When analyzing the key elements of a crime, law enforcement likes to consider the means, the opportunity, and the motive. Thus, a jealous husband (motive) who owns a gun (means) and is alone with his rival (opportunity) becomes a logical suspect when that rival is murdered. Translating this into the context of undercover conversational strategies, the opportunity is when a cooperating witness or agent meets with the target, the motive is when the target says something incriminating, and the obvious means to do this is the way language is used by the target.

The very presence of these three key elements heightens the language consciousness of the persons wearing the mike and makes them aware that they may need to use certain language strategies consciously in order to meet their goals, particularly when the targets are not self-generating their own guilt. For this reason, I aver that most conversational strategies used by persons who know the significance of the tape they are producing are, indeed, deliberately carried out.

This book describes twelve actual cases in which alleged crimes were actually created by the use of various conversational strategies employed by law enforcement and its representatives, where no such crime is actually indicated by the language evidence. In two of these cases (chapters 7 and 10), at the request of attorneys and their clients, the real names and places are fictionalized to protect the privacy of the targets.

2

Conversational Strategies Used to Create Crimes

Following Tannen (1994), I use the term, "conversational strategy," to refer simply to a way of speaking. We don't find a great deal about conversational strategies in the linguistic literature. Linguists are more concerned about forms, patterns, and rules, while people tend to associate strategies more with warfare, sports, or business plans. Many scholars who do study discourse strategies tend to think of them as unconscious (Tannen 1994) or automatic (Gumperz 1982) language manifestations. However, since the goal of language is to communicate, it is reasonable to believe that there are times when strategic conversational goals are used deliberately and by conscious choice. Hansell and Ajirotutu (1982) recognize such possibilities, describing discourse strategies as "ways of planning and negotiating the discourse structure (conversational agenda) over long stretches of conversation" (87).

In everyday conversation, when the cooperative principle of conversation is working well (Grice 1975), conversational strategies may indeed be automatic or unconsciously used. But when the conversation is planned well in advance, has a specific result in mind, and is being secretly recorded for posterity by one of the participants, there is a better than average chance that the choice of discourse strategies by the person wearing the mike is very conscious indeed. Craig and Tracy (1983) seem to be clear about how such strategies can be deliberate when they report:

A "strategic" account of coherence . . . would assume that conversationalists behave strategically in pursuit of their individual goals, and that whatever structure conversation may have emerges from this process. Rules and standard patterns are not simply followed but are used as resources to accomplish goals. Rules may be broken, transformed, or used in non-obvious ways. Or if rules are followed strictly, as in a sport or game, they may be only a constitutive framework in which non-rule governed strategic options are played out. (15)

Whether used consciously or unconsciously, the result may be called a strategy when it can be identified linguistically, when it is patterned, and when it is repeated. When conversational strategies can be identified and named, they have an existence that must be noticed, especially in criminal cases where the stakes of personal freedom are very high. During the past twenty-five years I have reviewed thousands of undercover tape recordings in hundreds of criminal cases. On many of these tapes, certain conversational strategies gave every evidence of being used consciously by the person wearing the mike. In the context of these cases, it is relatively certain that this conscious use accomplished a specific conversational goal, namely to create the illusion that the targets had agreed to or had participated in the past in illegal activities when the actual language used on those tapes did not support the illusion being created. In other words, the alleged crime was cleverly created by the person wearing the mike.

The question of intentionality rears its head here. Did the undercover agents and the cooperating witnesses intend to create such an illusion? Was it their major agenda? One can expect better from police interrogators and certainly from prosecutors, who operate in a somewhat different context. But there can be only one agenda for undercover agents wearing the mike—to capture illegality on tape. Although they may try to deny this, there can be no other reason for taping a target in the first place. I have testified to this fact many times at trial and the obviousness of my claim has never been challenged successfully. This is important to be said early and often because it underlines the linguistic analysis of the taped conversation. In their effort to capture crime on tape, people wearing the mike often employ certain conversational strategies, such as the ones described here.

Many of the conversational strategies used by law enforcement officers that are described and illustrated in this book seriously affected the knowledge of the targets. Communication requires a definable amount of *shared* knowledge in order to provide the context necessary for participants to understand what is being said to them. These targets used conventional inferences and situated contextualization cues as the basis for interpreting what they mistakenly considered shared knowledge when, in contrast, it was often not shared at all.

The following is a description of eleven conversational strategies that cooperating witnesses and agents have used to create the illusion of a crime when one was not otherwise happening. In this chapter, some brief examples are taken from specific undercover tape operations in the past. Chapters 4 through 15 will describe twelve criminal cases in more detail, showing how one or more of these strategies played out in more recent real-life undercover conversations.

1. Using Ambiguity

People can be ambiguous or vague without intending to be so, but when they use ambiguity deliberately, it can help create the appearance of a crime in a conversation that isn't actually there. Ambiguity decreases the possibility of the participants attaining shared knowledge.

Nobody can know for sure, of course, exactly what another person's intentions are, but when a speaker has the opportunity and ability to say something clearly, yet chooses not to do this on multiple critical occasions, there is a strong likelihood that the ambiguity is a purposeful strategy to keep the listener from knowing exactly what is meant.

There are many ways such ambiguity can be created. A common example is when we use words such as "it," and "the thing" without identifying the noun antecedents to "it" and "the thing." In chapter 4, for example, we will see how a cooperating witness says he will "do" several people for the target. He could have said "kill," but instead he chose to use the vague dummy verb. In the context of this case, the target had previously asked the cooperating witness to spy on these people, like a private investigator, in order to determine whether or not they were in a secret sexual tryst. In much of life's conversations, such ambiguity can be tolerated, but criminal evidence requires a great deal more explicitness. The possibility of alternative understandings is simply too important.

Labov (2003) argues that much of narrative analysis starts with the assumption that "speakers transform reality by techniques more subtle and effective than lying" (74). Using the analysis of underlying event structure, Labov shows how a defendant at his trial in South Africa used one type of ambiguity to transform his account of the crucial events in order to minimize his own involvement in a series of murders. Among other things, the defendant admitted that he "fired at" the victim, but not that his bullet hit him. He then described how it was his partner who slit the victim's throat. "To fire at" normally presupposes that the defendant missed the target. The defendant also admitted that he "heard" his partner slam a door, which has the conversational implicature that he didn't "see" this happen. Hearing this testimony, the court was faced with the ambiguity of who actually killed the victim.

Another classic example of how ambiguity was used by a cooperating witness is the case of *United States v. John Z. DeLorean*, the millionaire carmaker (Shuy 1993). In the pivotal tape of the investigation, the cooperating witness used the noun, "investment," in an ambiguous way that did not specify who was investing in whom. In the overall context of some sixty previous conversations, DeLorean's words indicated that he believed that this meant that the undercover cooperating witness was agreeing to invest in the financially troubled DeLorean Motor Company. Ignoring this overall context, the prosecutor believed that in this conversation DeLorean meant that he was agreeing to invest in the cooperating witness's illegal drug operation. Neither party clarified this distinction in the tape upon which the government based its criminal case. This was not only faulty intelligence gathering by the cooperating witness, but it was also faulty intelligence analysis by the prosecution, and the government paid the price when DeLorean was acquitted of all charges.

2. Blocking the Target's Words

Conversation is sometimes like a basketball game, with both an offense and a defense. The aim is to score your own points (the offense) and to block the other speaker from making his or hers (the defense). Basketball defense is often accomplished by blocking the other team's shots and by intercepting its passes. Such strategies are conscious and deliberate ones that can change the appearance of the overall game. In conversations, such blocking can be accomplished in at least four ways: by creating static noise on the tape in places that appear to be exculpatory, by interrupting or overlapping the target's voice in crucial passages, by answering on behalf of the target, and by turning the recorder off whenever the target seems to be trying to say something exculpatory.

a. Creating static on the tape

The persons wearing the hidden microphone have control and power over what is being recorded. They can even move away from a conversation if it isn't going the way they want it to go. Many mikes are sensitive to movement sounds and produce a kind of static noise when the wearers move around. If they chose to move at a crucial point, the resulting noise can successfully block on tape what the target is saying. This strategy was used in several of the conversations described below, but especially in chapter 9.

b. Interrupting or overlapping the target's words

Another strategy is to verbally block what the target is beginning to say, either by interrupting the target, blocking him from going on, or by overlapping the target's words, making it difficult, if not impossible, for later listeners to the tape to understand the target's words. For example, if targets appear to be disagreeing with a questionable hint or a blatantly illegal expression uttered by the cooperating witness or agent, this disagreement can be blocked by verbally interrupting or talking over the targets' voices.

Interrupting is noticed by practically everyone. One example of this is found in the letters of Abigail Adams to her husband John Adams during the days at or around the American Revolution. Abigail complained about the tendency of New Yorkers to interrupt constantly: "They talk very loud, very fast, and altogether. If they ask a question, before you can utter three words of your answer, they will break out upon you again—and talk away" (McCullough 2001, 25).

Despite the universality of interruption and overlap, its significance in a criminal case is often overlooked in the legal system. People interrupt each other for a number of possible reasons, including strong disagreement with what was said by the other person, lack of interest in what is being said, or simply from extrovertish habits of domination. People also interrupt when they agree and are impatient to get on with the subject and try to lead it to some conclusion. In some groups, especially among certain females, interruption can also be a sign of cooperation and solidarity (Tannen 1994), but I have not found this to be the case in the hundreds of criminal cases I've analyzed. Not surprisingly, the prosecution and defense may see such interruption in quite different ways, if they even notice it at all.

c. Speaking on behalf of the target

In some cases the strategy of interruption escalates even further. The agent not only blocks the targets' turns of talk, but also usurps that turn to speak on their behalf. One of the things we assume in conversation is that the one who has something to say is the one who says it. In a conversation when one person speaks on behalf of another, Schiffrin calls it "speaking for another" (1993). Tannen's (2004) term for this is "ventreloquizing," a discursive strategy by which a participant speaks in the voice of a nonverbal party in the presence of that party. A common negative interpretation of this is called "butting in" while a more positive interpretation is considered "chipping in" and might be thought of as part of a display of politeness (Brown and Levinson 1987). In Goffman's terms, when one person speaks on behalf of another, that person assumes the role of the animator for the other person and takes on that person's role (1967). Sometimes, institutionally sanctioned rules permit this to happen, as when a parent speaks on behalf of a child or when a translator speaks on behalf of a foreign-language speaker. But in most conversations, speaking on behalf of another depends on current perceptions of alignments (Schiffrin 1993). Participant alignments are related to the way participants position themselves relative to each other, including their power and solidarity and their footing (Goffman 1979).

An example of speaking on behalf of another participant occurred in a criminal case involving New Jersey gaming casino commissioner Kenneth McDonald (Shuy 1993). An undercover FBI agent had already co-opted an unsuspecting New Jersey mayor in a bribery plot. The co-opted mayor then advised the agent that he knew how he could bribe Commissioner McDonald to get his favorable vote on a new casino project that the mayor and the agent were planning. One evening, the mayor invited McDonald to go with him to have dinner downtown, explaining that he would have to stop at the office along the way "to pick up something." That "something" turned out to be a briefcase full of cash that the mayor had already told the agent would be passed along to McDonald to assure his favorable vote. The FBI agent, unaware that McDonald knew nothing about the mayor's scheme, tried hard to involve McDonald in the conversation. Videotapes of this meeting show McDonald standing on the other side of the small office, looking out the window, unaligned with the conversation of the other two men, waiting for the mayor and the undercover agent to finish their business. Finally, exasperated at McDonald's seeming indifference, the agent turned directly to him and said:

> *Agent*: I hope, Ken, that there won't be any problem with you—
> *Mayor [interrupting and speaking on behalf of McDonald]*: No, there's no problem.
> *Agent [finishing his interrupted sentence]*: —licensing or anything in, uh, Atlantic City as a result of this.
> *Mayor [again answering on behalf of McDonald]*: Okeydokey, in regards to licensing, if I may just bring that point out, just recently I talked to him on the phone, so there's no question about that. You're in first place.

In addition to speaking on behalf of McDonald, note how the mayor and the agent used the ambiguous indexicals, "this" and "him," which, to McDonald, could well have referred to something and someone other than himself. After two more equally failed attempts to involve McDonald in the discussion, the agent concluded the conversation, once again trying to address McDonald directly:

> *Agent*: Thank you very much, Ken.
> *McDonald*: Good to see you and I'm sure—
> *Mayor [again interrupting and speaking for McDonald]*: I'm sure we'll do alright, huh?
> *Agent*: I don't—
> *Mayor*: [*interrupting the agent*]. Won't be any problems.
> *Agent*: No problems?

Mayor: No problems.
McDonald: I'm, I have nothing to do with that.

The curious thing about this case is that even though McDonald distanced himself from the conversation between the agent and the mayor by physically disaligning himself from them on the other side of the room and looking out the window, even though it was not McDonald making these statements, and even though he verbally disaligned himself by denying having anything to do with whatever it was the other two men were talking about, he was indicted just the same. This fact highlights the less than adequate way that people, including prosecutors, do not attend to blocking strategies that show the subtleties of interruption, overlap, ambiguous referencing, and speaking on behalf of the other person in everyday conversations.

d. Manipulating the on/off switch

Unscrupulous cooperating witnesses (there can be no doubt about the fact that most of these have already been caught in a crime themselves) sometimes have the power to decide when to tape-record and when to turn the recorder off. In fairness to law enforcement it should be said that in many effective undercover operations this problem is avoided by prefacing each recording with a prologue clearly stating when the tape was turned on and a postlogue statement stating when it was turned off. If the tape is turned off during the conversation, conscientious police officers also indicate this clearly on the tape. Undercover taping often produces long stretches containing the sounds of walking, driving, and other noncrucial events that are bothersome to wade through, but on-tape indications of when the tape is on and off ensure against the criticism of selectivity in taping and manipulation by the cooperating witness or person wearing the mike.

One of the cases described in this book (chapter 9) describes an undercover operation in Texas in which a convicted felon, acting as a cooperating witness, was given virtually unsupervised power for ten days, during which time he had the sole responsibility of deciding when to tape and when not to. There were no tape-recorded prologues or postlogues to indicate the times or even dates that the taping was made.

As a result, we can never know for sure what exculpatory passages were omitted from his taping.

This book is about undercover taping by both cooperating witnesses and law enforcement officers, but the principles are virtually the same when the police interrogate a suspect for several hours yet tape record only the final minutes in which a confession is obtained. In such interrogations, we have absolutely no evidence of what was said leading up to that confession. One of the most outrageous examples of manipulating the on/off switch that I have ever experienced was in the case of Jerry Townsend, a mentally retarded man accused of killing a number of prostitutes in the area of Dade and Broward counties, Florida (chapter 15). The police turned the recorder off and on in a highly questionable manner over a period of four days. For example, in one instance Townsend admitted that he had killed a black woman in a white Stingray automobile. The tape clicked off, coming on later with Townsend saying that it was a white woman in a white Sting ray. Satisfied that the suspect had finally gotten the facts to match the crime, the police then went on to elicit the next series of facts, which Townsend frequently got wrong again, at least until the tape was once again turned off, then back on. Of course we can never know exactly what happened during those many intermissions and corrections, but it is not difficult to suspect that the police coached him with the right answers while the tape recorder was turned off. Manipulating the tape recorder in this way makes it easier to create evidence of criminal acts that never existed.

All four of these types of conversational blocking reduce the possibility that later listeners, such as juries, will to be able to discover whether or not the agents and the targets shared the same knowledge about what was actually going on.

3. The Hit-and-Run Strategy

If the target does not say anything that seems to point to his guilt, many undercover operators begin to "drop in" hints about illegality, sometimes clear and sometimes not. It is commonplace that when they drop these hints into the conversation and are unsure how their targets might react, they often quickly change the subject to something benign before they give up their turn of talk. By the time the targets get a chance to say anything, they are most likely to respond to the newly changed subject, letting the hint slip by them without giving a response to it. They may not have even caught the hint at all.

Why would the target respond to the changed topic and not to the preceding hint of illegality? Linguists who study conversation have found such behavior to be rather normal. It is the result of what linguists call the recency principle. When given an uninterrupted series of questions or statements, listeners tend to respond only to the most recent or last one in the series.

One might argue that speakers are quite capable of changing their own topics midway through their turn of talk in a perfectly unconscious manner. This is quite true. The common occurrence of this undoubtedly contributes to the targets' lack of responses to the parts that are not the most recent. People talk like that all the time. But if the persons wearing the mike have the sole agenda of preserving this conversation for later listeners, such as juries, to hear, their awareness of what they are doing is likely to be heightened. Cooperating witnesses want to get something useful for their handlers in order to get the extra consideration they need for a lighter sentence sometime down the road. After all, they have produced some words with illegal overtones and it's right there on the tape for all to hear. The targets haven't objected to it (if they caught the hint at all), and it provides seemingly good material for the prosecution.

Whether the hit-and-run strategy is used by cooperating witnesses or by undercover police, the result is much the same and once again shared knowledge is not attained.

4. Contaminating the Tape

Some undercover operatives who try to make the tape look as bad as possible for the target have still another strategy to use. They know full well that later listeners are likely to believe that something illegal is going on. If the target's own words don't show this, there is also the possibility that the undercover operative can make the tape seem worse by contaminating it with some covert and bad-sounding language. It doesn't seem to matter that such language was not spoken by the target. Who will be able to keep straight who said what anyway?

Defendants in tape cases begin every trial with two strikes against them. Strike one is that they have been indicted for a crime. Strike two is that there are tapes that the prosecution claims will prove their guilt. It's hard for an innocent defendant to overcome these two strikes, since juries tend to believe that taped evidence is always bad. To ensure that they believe this, some cooperating witnesses and agents spice up the tape with references to other criminal activity (even if these are unrelated to this operation), drop in names of unsavory people, use questionable expressions, and try to talk like criminals, using vulgarity and cursing. No matter that the target doesn't use such language. It's on the tape and who can sort it out?

One example of the contamination strategy was seen in the Abscam case of U.S. Senator Harrison A. Williams of New Jersey in the early 1980s. After Senator Williams had made it very clear that any money he might be able to make on a proposed business deal would have to be legally declared as a blind trust, the FBI agent, Anthony Amoroso, kept saying that the senator would have to "keep it hidden." In one sense a blind trust would indeed be hidden, but hidden only *to* the senator, not *by* him. The damage was done, however, and despite the senator's clear words to the contrary, the prosecution claimed that he agreed to keep his potential earnings hidden (Shuy 1993). For some reason, the jury agreed with the prosecutor and Williams was convicted at trial.

Although I was not asked to participate in Senator Williams's criminal trial, I had a personal opportunity to witness such contamination later, during the senator's impeachment hearing in which I gave testimony. I sat next to Williams on the Senate floor and during one of the breaks in the hearing Senator Mark Hatfield of Oregon, whom I knew from the fact that we attended the same church, came up to us and asked Williams why he swore so much on the tape. The fact is that Senator Williams was *not* the one swearing on the tape. It was FBI Agent Amoroso. Even Senator Hatfield was contaminated by the tape recordings. As it turned out, the entire U.S. Senate was equally contaminated. Near the end of the hearings, since Senator Williams realized that he had not convinced many of his colleagues of his innocence, he resigned from the U.S. Senate.

5. Camouflaging the Illegality

This strategy is a form of deception in which the person wearing the mike represents something as perfectly legal when, in reality, it is not. The words used, the proposed actions, and the ultimate results are couched in legal terms even though it is clear to everyone but the target that they are not legal. This strategy is analogous to one used by some unscrupulous used-car salespersons to get the buyers interested enough to commit, then tell them that there are other costs that have to be added or that their trade-in vehicles are not worth what the customer originally was led to think. The target buys into the deal, at least initially, believing it to be a legitimate deal. At some point the customers may discover their error in judgment, but by then it's often too late and they become victims of the salesperson's trap.

This strategy is most common in cases involving allegedly illegal stock transactions and other types of business fraud. There is no way that any undercover operative employing this deceptive strategy upon a target can be excused for acting unconsciously. Camouflage is deliberate by its very nature. This strategy is often used as a way to get the target into a discussion until the agent's real motive, to make an actual representation of illegality, is slowly accomplished. At that point, of course, it behooves the target to say "no," but often far too many wheels are already in motion, making it increasingly difficult for the target to back out. In other areas of life this technique is referred to as "bait and switch." Shared knowledge may be eventually accomplished, but too late for some targets to stop.

6. Isolating Targets from Important Information

The most deliberate conversational strategy of all is one in which the targets are isolated from the information that they need in order to make a valid yes-or-no decision about getting involved in the proposed enterprise. Using this strategy, undercover operatives actually avoid and prevent the attainment of shared knowledge. Meetings or parts of meetings can be held outside the target's presence or the person wearing the mike can say something incriminatory, then physically move just far enough away from the target that any response, inculpatory or exculpatory, cannot be heard on the tape.

This strategy is common at important meetings in which crucial topics are discussed while the target is not present or not even invited, something that happened often in the bribery case of Senator Harrison A. Williams (Shuy 1993). However logical it might seem to those juries who listen to the tapes later that the target wasn't even present, such an insight doesn't happen very often. Later listeners often miss this important fact completely. They get confused easily about who said what to whom and when it was said. Clever and unscrupulous undercover operatives are aware of this. Their job is to get illegal talk on tape whether or not the target is present. Doing this also illustrates still another version of the contamination strategy, discussed above.

A variation of this strategy takes place when the persons wearing the mike utter the inculpatory statements after they notice that the target has moved to another physical location in the area. This happened to Hugo Forrester, a San Jose jeweler, when the cooperating witness noticed that Forrester was busy with another customer on the other side of the showroom (Shuy 1993). Careful listening to tape recordings of such conversations enables one to detect nonlanguage sounds that signal, in general, the distances the speakers are likely to be from each other, the sounds of footsteps, and the sounds of doors opening and closing. Audible language clues may also be noticed. If the targets are engaged in conversations with someone else at the time the critical words are spoken on the tape by the agent or cooperating witness, there is a pretty good chance that the targets weren't able to hear what the operatives were saying.

Other language clues to the target's presence or absence include the use of greeting and closing routines. We can be relatively certain that the targets *are present* when someone addresses them saying, "Hi Paul, how are you?" Another clue is found in the way pronouns are used. Second-person pronouns "you," "your," and "yours" give a clue that the target is being addressed while "he," "his," and "him" indicate that someone else is the addressee. Chapter 9 deals with these in more detail.

7. Ignoring the Target When He Says "No"

What do people really mean when they say "no"? Salespersons are very good at ignoring rejections by their customers, instead going right ahead in their efforts to make a sale. In the case of undercover operations one might also ask, "How many times does the target need to say "no" before the agent accepts this as the end of the investigation?"

In the FBI Abscam operation of the early 1980s Congressman Richard Kelly of Florida offered a functional "no" to FBI agent Tony DeVito eight times before finally accepting a twenty-five-thousand-dollar bribe to use his influence to help an alleged Arab sheik obtain U.S. citizenship, a clear and damaging quid pro quo. The prosecution could argue, perhaps effectively, that the agent realized that Kelly was disingenuous or coy as he turned the bribe down eight times before finally stuffing the money in his pockets. Or was Kelly in a state of confusion about what to do, being first inclined to say "no," then changing his mind as the incentive grew in value to him? Kelly's trial defense was that the more times the agent offered the bribe, the more he grew suspicious of that agent and decided that he would begin his own investigation of the operation by first accepting the money as evidence that the undercover agent was guilty of a bribery attempt. Not surprisingly, the jury did not buy this defense theory and Kelly was eventually convicted. The fact remains, however, that Kelly did turn down the offer verbally eight times before he finally knuckled under and accepted it. What role should persuasion play in undercover cases? If a target is genuinely disinclined at the beginning, is it appropriate for the agent to pursue anyway, like a persistent used-car salesperson? And can we accept the intuitions of agents who claim to be able to distinguish between the target's words of rejection and his intended willingness based on greed? Are agents really that perceptive? Is anyone?

8. Inaccurately Restating What the Target Says

I first discussed this conversational strategy as it was used by the agent in the bribery case of Senator Williams (Shuy 1993). I've since run into it in numerous other cases, including the money laundering case of Richard Silverman (Shuy 2001), when Silverman's references to Mexico were restated by the agent as "down south" and "Colombia," giving the appearance that Silverman was involved in money laundering for a drug dealer. Silverman's references to Mexico were to the flight capital of a man who was alleged to be an investor in Silverman's stock. Based on the language of the tapes, there was no good reason for the agent to have misunderstood Silverman. It would appear that the agent's inaccurate restatements were cutting corners, making Silverman look like something he was not. Inaccurate restatements of what the target has said are closely related to the strategy of contamination, noted earlier.

9. Withholding Crucial Information from the Target

In undercover operations the target must make an informed decision about whether or not to proceed with whatever illegal act is being discussed. Although this is important in all phases of life, the stakes are much higher when one's liberty is involved. In order to make informed decisions, targets must have the relevant information on which to base any future actions. When the agent or cooperating witness provides only part of the critical facts, any decision to act is potentially compromised. For example, in a money laundering sting in the Washington, D.C., area, a number of automobile dealers were charged with accepting cash payments for car purchases that allegedly originated from drug sales. The problem was that the agent posing as a customer did not represent verbally that this money was from his drug business. The only clues provided to the salespersons were the hip-hop demeanor, vague slang, and flashy attire of the undercover cop. From this, the prosecution expected the car salespersons to infer that the agent was a streetwise money launderer. Although the prosecution claimed that the clues to the agent's purpose could be easily guessed by the car dealers, they forgot that it is always the case that implied information is susceptible to more than one interpretation.

10. Lying to the Target about Crucial Information

In police interrogations it is perfectly legal for an undercover officer to lie and trick a suspect about such matters as whether or not incriminating evidence exists in the case (Inbau, Buckley, and Reid 1986, 216–19).

This type of lying is condoned because it can be helpful in eliciting a quick confession. In undercover operations, however, lying to the target can be counterproductive to a fair conviction. If it is unfair to withhold important information that might cause the target to reject carrying out an illegal act, giving him false information upon which to base his decision is arguably even more unfair. Although undercover cases are, by definition, deception at work, there is a line that must be drawn about the type of deception used.

The agent is obviously playing a deceptive role, using a false identity along with other deceptive factors. But the crucial facts upon which a possible conviction rest must not be manufactured, else the target will have to base his decisions on whether or not to bite on faulty assumptions and facts. In the Texas Brilab investigation, *State of Texas v. Billy Clayton* (Shuy 1993), for example, the cooperating witness explained to the Texas Speaker of the House that he didn't have to report the campaign contribution he was offered. This untrue and misleading deception could have led to still other charges against the target. It was fortunate for Clayton that he knew that this information was a lie. Before he got a chance to report it, however, he was arrested and indicted for bribery. At trial the truth came out and he was acquitted.

11. Scripting the Target

The best language crime evidence against a target is always his own words, what I have called self-generated guilt. When an agent or cooperating witness tells the target what to say, doubts can be cast on exactly how real or genuine any repetition of such language can be. Citing the Abscam case of Senator Williams once more, FBI agent DeVito, along with cooperating witness Mel Weinberg, spent thirty minutes preparing the senator for an upcoming meeting with the alleged Arab sheik who was actually an undercover agent posing in that role. Their advice was for the senator to puff and brag about his rank in the Senate and how he had the power to move the process of getting a bill through Congress to provide the sheik with U.S. citizenship (Shuy 1993). In short, the senator was scripted in how to further a criminal act. The fact that he did not do this when he met with the alleged sheik appeared to be of no consequence to the jurors, however, who used this evidence to help convict him at trial.

A second type of scripting is not often recognized as such, but in many ways it has the same effect. When speakers ask other speakers what they should say to someone else (as in, "Tell me what I should say to my boss?"), we think of it as a request for a directive, which, of course, it is. Simultaneously, however, it is also a request for scripting. I am using the strategy of scripting here to include both "Here's what you should say" types of utterances as well as "What do you want me to say" types. Both encourage another person to provide words that are to be used.

In recent years we have witnessed considerable criticism of parents and even child-protection team workers who script and coach children who were the alleged victims of sexual abuse (Ceci and Bruck 1995; Poole and Lamb 1998). It has taken us a bit longer to understand that such coaching and scripting can also take place in undercover sting operations.

I want to be very clear that I am not saying that all undercover operatives and police interviewers use these eleven powerful conversational strategies unfairly. But I am saying that when these strategies are used, they can play a very important role in creating the appearance of a crime for which the target eventually is accused. Part of the intelligence analysis in any criminal case begins by recognizing whether the crime was actually committed by the target or whether an illusion of a crime was created by the person wearing the mike. Good intelligence analysis should recognize these conversational strategies for what they really are before any attempt is made to indict or convict the target. To do otherwise invites the defense to point out the unfairness of these conversational strategies at trial, usually at the prosecution's expense.

3

The Power of Conversational Strategies

Many people think that if they only had more power, their lives would be a lot better. They tend to think that it's better to be in a position where they can make the decisions, influence the outcome, and control the context. Such power can lead to an unequal balance in who gets what and who doesn't. Following Foucault (1997), we define power as a set of potentials for change that can be variably exercised, resisted, and shifted around. There are many different kinds of power that are interrelated and intertwined, although some people may have one kind of power and others a different kind. An individual's ability to achieve and maintain power depends on some things that he or she cannot control, such as age, status, gender, role, ethnicity, value systems, and ideology. If a person falls short on one or more of these uncontrollables, he or she can develop and exercise power and change by using language effectively. Robin Lakoff put it very nicely: "Language is a change-creating force and therefore to be feared and used, if at all, with great care, not unlike fire" (1989).

On the surface it might seem that the power of conversational strategies is similar to the power of persuasion. Persuasive communication makes use of certain rhetorical, stylistic techniques such as argumentation, flattery, tautologies, repetition, paraphrase, purposeful semantic shifts, connotations, or neologisms. The goal of these rhetorical acts is to convince listeners by triggering certain behavioral patterns through the perlocutionary effects created on them. In persuasive rhetoric the listener has to understand what is said in order to be influenced by it. The persuader tries to make listeners understand, then give up their points of view and embrace those of the persuader.

In the conversational strategies discussed here, we deal with something quite different and somewhat closer to what Sornig (1989) calls manipulative seduction:

> seduction is an attempt to make people do things as if of their own impulse but really upon instigation from outside.
>
> Whereas the mechanisms of convincing and conviction obviously work mainly along cognitive argumentative lines, seduction, instead of trusting in the truth and/or credibility of arguments, rather exploits the outward appearance and seeming trustworthiness of the persuader. Seductive persuasion tries to manipulate the relationship that obtains or is to be established between the speaker and his hearer.

When being seduced, the listener does not understand the hidden intent of the seducer and, unlike persuasion, seduction does not require the listener to embrace the speaker's perspective.

Conversational strategies generally have not been thought of as techniques of rhetorical persuasion. Although they are closer to seduction, the conversational strategies described in this book go even beyond seduction of their immediate audience, since they are used to influence the understandings of people *other than* the persons to whom they are addressed and they focus in on a time frame that is *not the same as* the time frame in which they were spoken. In addition, these conversational strategies find their power in face-to-face dialogue rather than in single-person communication such as speeches, lectures, or other forms of monologic address. Like seduction, intelligibility by listeners about what speakers say to them is the not same as it is in persuasive acts. In fact, just the opposite is true.

Perhaps the most commonly recognized function of language power resides in the speakers' ability to effectively implement their own agendas (Honneth 1991) and to dominate the agendas of other speakers (Burbules 1986). The most opportune time to call forth one's power is when there is a conflict of interest, in which case power relationships can be negotiated by the participants. In the undercover tape events described in this book, however, shared knowledge of the conflict of interest is not always held by the targets. In fact, the powerful speakers often depend on their power not being recognized, which is one reason why they create it through otherwise benign-looking conversational strategies. Doing so creates a blinding power, a power that is recognized only by one of the participants. Powerful speakers may exert power through language but their targets are not even aware of its significance, or often even of its existence.

Ainsworth-Vaughn (1998) describes the process of constructing power, which she claims has two components. The first is the basis for power negotiation. Structural power arises from the speaker's affiliation with a social institution. In her research, this social institution is the medical profession, since it has the power to prescribe drugs and treatment, over which the doctor has legitimate institutional authority. In the undercover cases described in this book, the social institution equivalent to the authority of a physician is not made apparent to the targets. The actual power of the social institution of law enforcement is not revealed to targets as the undercover operatives take on other identities that give the appearance of a more balanced social structure.

Ainsworth-Vaughn's second component in constructing power relationships is the discourse means for claiming power and control. Speakers' rights are related to social identity, their own and that of other participants, as well as to their understanding of the genre of the event. Talk, the major ingredient with which to do this, includes the rights to orderly turn taking, to introduce topics, to be able to get a point across, and to hold the floor. In the undercover cases described in this book, the targets are often kept uninformed of the real genre of their conversations and, as will be shown, the undercover agents use eleven conversational strategies to gain power over their targets.

A large proportion of linguistic research on powerful and powerless language has produced lists of features that characterize a speaker's *lack* of power. For example, the language of a less powerful speaker tends to employ more hedges, intensifiers, tag questions with rising intonation, hesitations, certain deictic phrases, and politeness forms (Lakoff 1973; O'Barr 1982; Ng and Bradac 1993). More powerful speakers are said to *not* use such forms as frequently, if at all. Although this finding may be accurate, it would seem that we might also identify some discrete language features that *powerful* speakers use other than the well-recognized power of the question asker. The eleven conversational strategies discussed in this book evidence ways that the speakers deliberately exerted their power by

- being ambiguous to targets, causing them to misunderstand and therefore give the appearance of guilt;
- blocking targets through interrupting and overlapping their speech, as well as blocking them electronically;
- bringing up a topic, then changing it before the other person has a chance to respond;
- contaminating the tape with irrelevant things that give later listeners an impression of sleaze or illegality;
- camouflaging illegality with the appearance of legality;
- isolating targets from information that they need to know in order to make informed decisions;
- refusing to take the target's "no" for an answer;
- misstating something targets have said to make them appear to have said something illegal;
- withholding important information that the target needs to know in order to make a legitimate and legal decision;
- lying to targets about things that they need to know in order to decide whether to follow an illegal or a legal course of action;
- scripting targets to say things that would make them sound guilty.

The targets in most of the cases described in this book were not likely to be thinking much about whether they were the powerful or powerless participants, while the undercover agents' probably were quite aware of this. The undercover agents had to be fully aware that their undercover roles assigned to them the right to disguise their power in the form of everyday conversation. The targets didn't know they were being recorded for later listeners to judge what they said and most of them had no idea of the ultimate significance of their conversations. They thought they were engaged in the conversational frame of familiar, normal talk, one that contained a more equal distribution of power. In short, the targets thought they understood what was really going on when often they did not.

Tannen describes a frame as the participants' understanding of the type of speech activity that is underway (1987; 1993). When participants do not share the same frame, confusion and ambiguity are the likely result. For this reason, language contains what Goffman (1974) calls "keys" that enable people to interpret frames. Keys can be as simple as increasing loudness of voice, clearing one's throat, or more complex keys that set the tone of the entire event, such as expressions of concern, expressions of anger, the use of sentence stress, or the occurrence of paralinguistic features such as laughing or crying (VanDijk 1985). These constitute metamessages or, in Bateson's terms, "framing devices" (1972). When such keys are conventionally used, they are meant to systematically transform an already meaningful message in a way that can be interpreted correctly. Participants are meant to comprehend the cues to the keying taking place (Goffman 1974). When they miss these keys, trouble begins.

Although there is no physical hitting or shoving going on, disguised or covert language power can produce a similar form of bullying. The language bully is often harder to recognize than the more obvious physical bully. One reason for this can be found in the nature of directness and indirectness in speech. In most of life, powerful participants do not need to worry a great deal about being impolite, rude, or even inaccurate. They also have nothing to fear about being indirect or vague. This becomes openly apparent when they are wearing a hidden microphone and have the advantage of using indirectness and ambiguity at will.

As will be noted throughout this book, one big problem with the undercover operatives' indirectness is that it is quite capable of being misunderstood. At the very time when law enforcement is supposed to be clear about the basis for inculpation, the agents often gave only vague hints about what they meant. Since they were the powerful persons in the interactions (by virtue of their wearing and controlling the mike and preserving the conversations for other listeners, such as juries, to hear at a later time), they could risk being indirect and ambiguous whenever they chose to do so. In fact, they undoubtedly hoped that their indirect and ambiguous contributions would flush out responses that would show their targets to be guilty. As an undercover technique, this is not necessarily a questionable method, at least not at the onset of the operation. But after it becomes apparent that this use of ambiguity and indirectness fails to yield inculpatory responses, its use becomes increasingly questionable and can become ultimately unfair to the targets.

In this book I try to show how undercover operatives have used the power of indirectness, ambiguity, and other conversational power strategies as a change-creating force to provide the additional control that leads to unfairness in their recorded conversations. The indisputable single goal of undercover operations like the ones described here is to capture crimes on tape. When this happens fairly, the prosecutors win. However, when it does not happen fairly, prosecutors' claims that the language evidence actually proves that they won fairly can be overturned by careful linguistic analysis of what was actually said and heard. Cameron et al. (1999) offer a strong warning to the powerful who abuse their language power: "And we should not forget a further complication, that those who are dominated in particular social relations can and do develop powerful, oppositional discourses of resistance—feminism, Black power, gay pride . . ." (153). And Lakoff (1989) put it this way:

> Even one who has the upper hand and is an abuser of others will in turn be abused by someone still higher or more skilled, or by someone who possesses particular expertise. Only by learning what power is assigned and determined through linguistic structure, and what power is equitable, what not, can we work to develop fairer ways of communicating. Then, at last, we can stop being mystified and victimized by those who wield the power inherent in language. Then we can decide, in Humpty Dumpty's words, "which is to be the master." (23)

Most of the recent concerns about power in the legal setting have focused on the language that goes on in the courtroom (Harris 1984, 1994; Solan 1993; Stygall 1994; Conley and O'Barr 1998). The witness stand is an alien context for most non-lawyers, who find the abstract language, jargon, and intricate syntactic constructions hard to understand (O'Barr 1982; Philips 1985; Tiersma 1999; deKlerk 2003). The status and power of the person who asks the questions, such as a policeman in the interrogation, a lawyer in the courtroom, a doctor in the medical examination, or a teacher in the classroom, are well known and predictable. But the power of an undercover operative is often less obvious and therefore more troublesome, seductive, and ultimately unfair. Three crucial factors accompany the conversational strategies to exert power used by cooperating witnesses and police in undercover tape recordings:

1. The significance of what the targets say is unknown to them.
2. The audiences for whom the recordings of the conversations are made are known by the covert recorder but not by the targets.

3. The time at which the conversation takes place is not the future time for which it will be used by the covert recorders.

Most commonly in life we think we are aware of the underlying significance of our own conversations and who our real audience is. We are usually unaware that our spoken words will be preserved to be used against us at some later time. Yet this is exactly the predicament that faces targets in undercover stings. Not knowing that they are being recorded, targets tend to treat these conversations like any other dialogic event. Had they known that their words were being tape-recorded, they could have requested clarification whenever ambiguities arose, rather than letting unclear statements go by unchallenged, the way we all often do in everyday talk. Had they known that their conversations were being taped, they could have made sure that they responded in clear and precise ways, not leaving open for later interpretation any possibility of alternative misunderstandings. They also could have been more attentive to what was being said to them and could have avoided letting their minds wander to some other topic at those critical moments. They could have tried to parse more carefully the possible meanings of what was being said to them.

Although the focus of this book is only on undercover operations, it should be noted that interrogations of suspects made by law enforcement officers use most of the same power strategies, but not as frequently as they are used in undercover operations. One reason for this may be that fairness in police interrogations is likely to be enforced more stringently, at least as long as they are tape-recorded. When police interrogations are recorded on audio- or videotape, defense attorneys should be able to call attention to the same powerful conversational strategies used in undercover cases, such as how the police use ambiguities, inaccurate restatements of facts, sudden hit-and-run utterances, contamination by inserting irrelevant information, camouflaging illegality, scripting the defendant in what to say, and refusing to accept the defendant's multiple, consistent, and supportable denials of guilt. Unfortunately, not all defense attorneys are alert to the power of such conversational strategies and are usually untrained in how to discover and deal with them.

In courtroom exchanges, the language power of prosecutors is even more capable of being challenged, since defense attorneys are there to watch out for their clients and can object when the defendant is exposed to the ambiguities, interruptions, and inaccuracies sometimes used by prosecutors. It is common for defense attorneys to object to leading and multiple questions, but many of the conversational strategies discussed here slip right by them, unnoticed and without a formal objection. The way language is used to exert power is amply illustrated by Bollinger's (1980) examples of its application in politics, advertising, propaganda, and the media. Lakoff (2000) does much the same in her analyses of how power was used in the criminal court case of O. J. Simpson, in the hearings involving Justice Clarence Thomas's appointment to the U.S. Supreme Court, and in the public presentations of Hillary Clinton. Cotterill (2003) also painstakingly analyzes how language power was used in the O. J. Simpson case from the time of jury selection to the postacquittal aftermath, particularly how questions control answers in the courtroom and how lawyers carefully use their own metaphors, then reframe the metaphors used by the other side to suit their own purposes. These studies, along with Lakoff's *Talking Power* (1989), speak strongly about how linguistic analysis can help identify conversational power, how to discover ways in which such power can be used either equitably or inequitably, and how to create fairer ways of communicating. Since undercover operations offer a virtual workshop in the ways that conversational strategies are used to create a power imbalance with unfair consequences to the targets whose words can become twisted against them, these events are the focus of this book.

PART II

Uses by Cooperating Witnesses

This section describes actual criminal law cases in which cooperating witnesses wore the microphone in undercover operations. The focus is on the conversational power strategies of blocking by interrupting and overlapping, using ambiguity, not taking "no" for an answer, scripting the target by requesting directives and apologies, lying about crucial information that the targets would need in order to decide whether or not to continue, withholding information from the target that is provided to another participant, and contaminating the taped record with information that has nothing to do with the target or the case, but which makes the target appear to be guilty.

4

Overlapping, Ambiguity, and the Hit and Run in a Solicitation to Murder Case: *Texas v. T. Cullen Davis*

The legal troubles of the legendary wealthy oilman, T. Cullen Davis, were the everyday talk in Texas during the 1970s and 1980s. He had inherited a company worth half a billion dollars from his father, a hard worker who had built a very successful oil equipment business in Fort Worth. Unfortunately, Cullen had few of the characteristics of an effective business executive. His tastes tended more toward those of the working class and his decision making in business and personal matters was hardly to be admired. It's hard to tell the truth from the legends, but it was rumored that Davis's second wife, Priscilla, may have been a former prostitute and that his wedding gift to her was a necklace with the words, "rich bitch," spelled out in diamonds. But this marriage didn't go well and the couple soon separated, with Priscilla staying in their Fort Worth mansion after Cullen had moved out.

On August 2, 1976, at the Davis mansion, a masked intruder broke in and killed Priscilla's live-in boyfriend, Stan Farr, along with her twelve-year-old daughter, Andrea, the product of an earlier marriage. Priscilla, who suffered only a gunshot wound to the breast, survived and immediately accused Davis of the murders. Two people who claimed to have seen the masked intruder leave the mansion supported Priscilla's accusation and Davis was arrested later that same night. The prosecutor decided to try Cullen for Andrea's murder first, thinking that if Davis were tried for the murder of his wife's lover, the jury might be more sympathetic to his defense. The testimony of Priscilla and the two witnesses was to no avail, however, and about a year later in an Amarillo courtroom, a jury acquitted Davis of the charge of murdering Andrea after only four hours of deliberation.

The saga didn't stop with Davis's acquittal, however. Nine months later, while the divorce proceedings were progressing slowly, Davis became convinced that Priscilla was intimate with the judge who was handling their divorce case. Davis claimed that he called on one of his midlevel employees, David McCrory, to tail the couple and get the goods on them. But McCrory's story was very different. He went to the police and told them that Davis had confessed to the murders and had asked him to find someone to kill the judge and Priscilla, along with the witnesses who were in the area at the time of the murders and who had identified Davis as the killer. McCrory also said that Davis threatened to kill him if he didn't carry out his requests.

FBI agents were called in and they decided to wire McCrory up and get him to engage Davis in conversations to prove that he wanted McCrory to hire an assassin to do the job. After four such conversations were tape-recorded by McCrory, the prosecutor thought he had all the evidence he needed. Davis was indicted again and a trial was held in Houston. It yielded only a hung jury.

Prosecutor Jack Strickland was undaunted by the hung jury in this solicitation to murder trial. He still claimed that Davis had the motive and opportunity, even though the means, the gun, was never discovered. He again lined up Priscilla and the eyewitnesses who claimed they saw the masked man leave the house. They all still swore that it was Davis. More important, he still had McCrory's tape-recorded conversations upon which he could try once more to succeed in his prosecution. Maybe a different jury would think differently about it. In the fall of 1979 the retrial began.

It was a very slow-moving process, lasting some six months, and filled with theatrics on both sides. Among other things, the government produced photographs of one of the people Davis was allegedly seeking to have had murdered, the divorce trial judge, poised curled up in the trunk of a car with fake blood all over his back. The prosecutor claimed that these photographs were shown to Davis during one of the conversations, although Davis denied ever seeing them. At the last of the taped meetings, McCrory was alledged to have shown the pictures to Davis to prove that he had indeed hired the killer that Davis allegedly requested, but the words used never seemed to make this clear. Throughout the trial Davis's famous criminal defense attorney, Richard "Racehorse" Haynes, engaged in daily verbal squabbles with prosecutor Jack Strickland, both inside and outside the courtroom. It was a true media event for the Texas newspapers, radio, and television.

A month into the trial, I was sitting in the middle seat on a flight from Washington, D.C., to Dallas. I couldn't help seeing what the man next to me was reading. To me it looked like a sermon, so I asked him if he was a minister. He laughed as he said he was the attorney defending a Dallas preacher in a civil suit. He then asked me what I did for a living and I replied that I was a linguist who analyzed tape-recorded speech. This answer usually produces stony silence, but this lawyer seemed oddly excited. He told me that his attorney-colleague had a case in Fort Worth where tape recordings were the primary evidence. He asked for my business card and I thought that would be the end of the matter. But a few days later I received a phone call from one of the attorneys assisting Racehorse Haynes in the Davis case, asking me to come there to talk about how I might help them. He then sent me the tapes in the case and my career as a forensic linguist was launched. Sometimes mere chance meetings change the directions of one's life. This was one of them for me.

One of the things I discovered from the tape recordings was that Davis never initiated any topics about soliciting murder. It was always McCrory who brought such topics up, and not very explicitly at that. He proposed "doing" Priscilla and "doing" the judge, a verb that would later be challenged by the defense, since Haynes argued that "doing" meant spying on them in an investigatory manner. It would seem that McCrory was deliberately ambiguous here, trying to make the tape look like Davis was not objecting to his "doing" these people. I also noticed that when McCrory seemed to suggest "doing" Priscilla and the judge, Davis was either totally silent or uttered off-topic answers, hardly evidence of his enthusiasm for a murder.

In October 1979 I arrived in Fort Worth to testify as an expert witness in the case. It was my first experience on the witness stand and I didn't really know what to expect. Haynes and I had discussed how my direct examination would go, but when he began to question me in court I could see that he was going in some quite different directions.

He led me through my topic analysis showing that the topic of killing anyone was never introduced by Davis. I opined that this was somewhat surprising if murder for hire was Davis's actual agenda. Equally helpful to Davis was that his responses to McCrory's statements that he would "do the judge" and "do Priscilla" were a combination of stony silence and coughs. I could show from the tape that Davis did not offer agreement to McCrory's proposals, regardless of whether he interpreted them as investigatory "doing" or killing. Davis didn't disagree either, but just uttered noncommittal grunts if anything at all.

The most crucial tape of all, the last one, contained one passage at the end that the newspapers had already printed over and over again. Before this fourth conversation was taped, McCrory's supervising agents had probably noticed that up to that time he had not been explicit about what he meant by "doing" Priscilla and "doing" the judge. To strengthen their case, McCrory was probably instructed to use the words, "kill," or "murder" in his follow-up meetings with Davis. McCrory must have had a hard time with this instruction, but he did manage to use the expressions, "I got judge Eidson dead," and "you want a bunch of people dead." The newspapers printed the prosecution's transcript, which went like this:

> *McCrory*: I got Judge Eidson dead for you.
> *Davis*: Good.
> *McCrory*: I'll get the rest of them for you. You want a bunch of people dead, right?
> *Davis*: Alright, but—

The newspapers' rendering of the government transcript stopped here but it could well have included the words of both men immediately following:

> *McCrory*: Help me too.
> *Davis*: I got to have an alibi ready for Art when the subject comes up. So give me some advance warning.
> *McCrory*: I will. I gotta go.

Even the defense team agreed that this passage did not look good for Davis but it struck me as odd that the intonation and pace of Davis's responses, "Good," and "Alright," were hardly enthusiastic reactions to McCrory's questions. The timing of these responses was also not quite right. In addition, Davis's statement about Art seemed strangely irrelevant to me in this snippet of the conversation. Art was McCrory's boss at Davis's company. If McCrory had already gotten somebody else to do the killing, as he claimed, why was it necessary to have an alibi ready for Art? McCrory's work, that of allegedly finding a hit man, would have been over by that time. He wouldn't really need a continuing excuse for missing work. I didn't find out until after the trial that Davis claimed to have asked McCrory to spy on the behavior of Priscilla and the judge, which fact could have explained why Davis was telling McCrory that he needed to give Art an alibi for his employee's absence from his job.

My direct examination went on for two long days, much of it consisting of almost constant arguments between the attorneys, and sidebars at the bench—sometimes when the jury was sent out of the room while points of law and procedure were discussed. When Racehorse Haynes had finally finished with my direct examination, I realized that he hadn't brought up the critical passage about getting the judge and others dead, for which I was primed to give a helpful analysis. I thought Haynes had forgotten about it, which was disappointing, since I had spent hours listening to the tape and had prepared my own transcript and chart of it, clearly showing something very different from what the newspapers had printed.

On the third day of my testimony, prosecutor Jack Strickland began to cross-examine me. One of the first questions he asked me was about this passage. "I noticed, Dr. Shuy, that your testimony said nothing about the passage talking about getting Judge Eidson and others dead." Relieved that I now had a chance to talk about it, I replied, "I've made a chart of this for the jury if you'd like to see it now." Strickland now couldn't say that he didn't want to see it so I brought out my chart of this same passage. And then I suddenly realized that Haynes deliberately had not asked me about this chart so that he could set a trap for Prosecutor Strickland to fall into. To say that the prosecutor was disarmed by this would be putting it mildly.

I explained to the jury that this part of the conversation was very rapid-fire and that sometimes both men were talking at the same time. Many listenings on high-quality equipment enabled me to report everything that was said, even when simultaneous, overlapping talk occurred.

There had also been a videotape made of this meeting, taken from a van parked across the parking lot from the car in which Davis and McCrory were sitting. The sound quality of the videotape was very poor but there was enough on it to serve as a touchstone reference for the audiotape made from McCrory's hidden mike. This videotape was not much discussed at trial, since the audiotape apparently seemed more audible and useful. But the video proved to be crucial to understanding what was really going on. Most important, it showed that at this point in the conversation, Davis got out of the car and went to the trunk, as he said on tape, to get his sunglasses.

My chart of this same passage picked up at the point of the topic that was being discussed before the "I got Judge Eidson dead for you" statement was uttered by McCrory. Context is always important in conversation analysis, as I've found in virtually every case I've worked on. How central the topic was is evident from my chart, which arranged the conversation in a form that was new to everyone, including the jury.

First, it had two columns rather than the conventional play script's single column that indicates discrete turns of talk. When there is a lot of overlapped speech, this two-column approach is obviously preferable. Second, it placed brackets around all of the simultaneous speech so that the jury could note what was actually being said simultaneously. Finally, it also noted the action, location, and movement of the two men, as revealed by the videotape.

Davis	McCrory
I told him that, uh, to treat you like any other employee and, uh, so don't give me too much pressure in that regard. I can't, uh, say you're gonna be gone a day or two every week or so.	
	(Davis gets out of the car and walks to the trunk.)
	Well look, this fuckin' murder business—
You better—	
	—is a tough son of a bitch.
alright,	
	Now you got me into this
[give me]	[into this goddamn deal]

[give me]	[right?]
a little	
[noti-, advance notice]	[Now I got j-]
	I got Judge Eidson dead for you
good [inaudible],	
	I'll get the rest of them dead
	for you. You want a bunch of
	people dead, right?
alright but I	
[uh, you know]	[di-, di-]
	Help me too,
[inaudible]	[okay?]
I got to have an alibi ready for	
Art when the-	
	Okay?
when the subject comes	
[up]	[alright]
(*Davis comes back to the front door of the car.*)	
So give me some advance notice,	
	I will.
warning.	
	I gotta go.
(*McCrory gets out of the car and leaves.*)	

It has been correctly pointed out that the evidence is the tape recording, not the written transcript of it. Yet when there is poor audibility, movement of the speakers, and overlapping speech, the average juror cannot possibly process all the information on an audiotape. In such cases, a guide to their listening is essential. With my transcript in hand, the jury listened to this passage several times and could better understand what was previously confusing to them.

I asked the jury to read down the speech of each separate column along with me and I pointed out that there were two different but simultaneous conversations about two different topics going on here. I showed them that immediately before and during this passage, Davis's conversational topic was about McCrory's boss, Art, and Davis's worries about McCrory missing too much work. At the very same time, McCrory's topic was about getting people dead. Both speakers stayed consistently on their separate topics. But McCrory's words about getting people dead were not spoken until Davis was outside the car and walking to the trunk.

But how could such a confusing conversation happen? Usually when both speakers talk about different things at the same time, one of them stops and tries to reconstruct some kind of topic unity. This didn't happen here. Why not? Here is where the much-overlooked videotape came in. There was just enough audibility on the audio track of the videotape to correlate it with McCrory's body mike audiotape. Since Davis was talking about Art (at the beginning of this chart), then suddenly opened the car door and began walking to the car's trunk to get his sunglasses, McCrory quickly took advantage of Davis's distance from his own body mike. It was at this point that McCrory spoke the damaging words about getting the judge dead and getting a bunch of people dead. Could Davis have heard this? If he did, his words didn't betray as much. He continued on with his own topic, about McCrory missing too much work. The damning words, "good," and "alright," were said in the context of giving an alibi to Art, not as a response to what McCrory was saying. Neither was uttered in a response intonation, but rather as low-pitch discourse markers related to his own topic.

The transcript upon which the government relied had at least some of the words spoken by Davis on it. The prosecution's transcribers did not have the skill or equipment to deal with the overlapped speech and since they listened only to the audiotape, they could not know that a physical separation between the two men had taken place. They could hear McCrory's voice better, of course, since the mike was attached to his chest. It was only by chance that Davis's "good" and "alright" fell into the slots of apparent agreement with what McCrory was saying. A complete rendering of what was said showed the government's transcript to be inaccurate. Davis talked about Art while McCrory muttered murder into the mike hidden under his shirt.

It stretches the imagination to believe that McCrory finally managed here to clarify his earlier "doing" the alleged victims to "getting them dead." It is noteworthy that this alleged clarification occurred at the only time in all the taping that Davis was out of hearing range. I have never understood what McCrory had to gain by manipulating the tape recording in this way. Apparently he was not a cooperating witness in the usual sense of the term. He did not agree to do this taping as a way of reducing the length of a prison sentence. In fact, as far as I know, he was not accused of anything. But, all the same, he was guilty of creating an alleged language crime. The tape fooled the prosecution into pursuing the trial and it almost fooled the jury into convicting Davis, based only on the illusion of criminality. But my explanation above convinced the jury that it was witnessing McCrory's manipulation of Davis's physical and auditory absence. McCrory created a language crime out of whole cloth by waiting until Davis got out of the car and was out of clear hearing distance to mutter the murder words into the mike.

This conversation also provides a classic example of how McCrory used the "hit-and-run" strategy. After he put what he considered the allegedly incriminating words on the tape, McCrory quickly ran away, saying "I gotta go." Even if Davis had been able to hear what McCrory was saying, he would not have had the opportunity to respond to it.

It was said that the Davis case was one of the most expensive ever tried in Texas. He had spent over ten million dollars on his defense and it is unknown how much it cost the state to prosecute him unsuccessfully at three different trials. Such an expenditure by the defendant can only happen when the client is very wealthy, raising the question of how well our justice system really works. A poor client could probably not have been able to afford the expert investigators and defense team that Davis was privileged to have.

5

Retelling, Scripting, and Lying in a Murder Case: Florida v. Alan Mackerley

Language crimes, or ones that are alleged to have happened, often occur before the tape-recording is even started. An event such as a solicitation to murder occurs and somebody tells the police about it. Since there is no tangible language evidence that the solicitation took place, the police wire up the persons who reported it to them and send them back to the solicitor to try to get him to retell it, this time on tape. If the retell strategy doesn't work well, a second related strategy is sometimes used, getting the target to tell the undercover taper exactly what to say. If the scripting strategy doesn't work, the strategy of planting false information is sometimes used next.

There are several problems with using the retell strategy, not the least of which is the believability of the request. The target might ask why the questioner would need or want to have any allegedly incriminating stuff repeated. Obviously, law enforcement needs the plot to be repeated more explicitly. So one strategy is for the undercover taper to request additional information about what the murder solicitor needs or wants, such as where the killing could best be accomplished, how it should take place, what the crime scene should look like, or how much pay will be involved. If the target bites on such matters, and possibly even reveals what was said earlier, before the taping began, the police have a solid case.

In some cases, however, all these matters were revealed in the initial meeting, the one that was not tape-recorded. If this happens, one conversational strategy is to try to get the target to retell what he said the first time. This requires the taper to claim having a bad memory or confusion about some things. Believability is clearly an issue for the solicitor unless there are conditions that make such memory loss seem genuine. One such condition is that the whole issue is thought to be very complicated. Another is that a long time has elapsed since the first discussion took place. Both can be feasible in some cases, as they were in the case of Alan Mackerley.

Then there is always the scripting strategy to use if the retell doesn't work effectively. And if that also fails, one can always plant some false information and see how the target responds to it. All three strategies are illustrated in the Mackerley case.

Mackerley was the long-time owner of a school transportation business in Sussex County, New Jersey. One of his competitors in this business was Frank Black. Mackerley and Black had been fighting over their respective school bus territories for some thirty years and had become bitter enemies. In 1996 Mackerley tried to buy out Black's bussing business. During this process, he enlisted his girlfriend, Lisa Costello, to go to Florida to try to sell some old school buses for export overseas. While Costello was there, she met Frank Black, who was there on similar business. They are alleged to have had a brief flirtation and suddenly Black went missing. No physical forensic evidence was ever discovered, including Black's body. Strangely enough, Costello also disappeared for a while. When she reappeared, she was questioned and her refusal to cooperate landed her a contempt of court citation with jail time.

The police were baffled by the case and it remained unsolved until Bill Anderson appeared on the scene. He was a former United Airlines pilot who had made a fortune in various recent businesses. Anderson and Mackerley had been best friends for years, but their relationship had become strained when Anderson learned that his wife and Mackerley had carried on an affair for some ten years. Not surprisingly, they then drifted apart until after Black's disappearance in 1996, when Anderson made a surprise visit to Mackerley. After this visit, Anderson went to the police, claiming that Mackerley had told him that he had flown to Florida, lured Black to his house, and shot him. The problem for the police was that it would be Anderson's word against Mackerley's, a situation that prosecutors fear most, sometimes called "a pissing match." They also feared that Mackerley's former affair with Anderson's wife might even appear to be the justification for Anderson to use this affair as a way to get even with Mackerley by making a false claim in the case. Both fears were well grounded.

Despite these qualms, the police were naturally intrigued by what Anderson told them, so they instructed him to meet with Mackerley to try to get him to repeat his alleged admission that he was the one who had killed Black. Anderson, of course, wore a hidden microphone during the meeting, which took place at Mackerley's home on August 29, 1996. Based on the audiotaped recording that Anderson made, Mackerley was indicted and tried for murder. The trial in 2001 ended with a hung jury. Shortly afterward, Anderson claimed that Mackerley had put out a hit on him. Anderson was subsequently placed into the witness protection program. The prosecution then retried the case in February 2003 in Clearwater, Florida, with Anderson and his tape recording as the only evidence. Gerald Krovatin, Mackerley's attorney at both trials, enlisted me to analyze the tape for the retrial.

The Retell Strategy

The police created a scenario for Anderson to use when he met with Mackerley the second time. He was to claim that he had been interviewed twice by the police and, as he put it to Mackerley, "they asked me some tough questions" in the second interview. Anderson was also coached to claim that he was in trouble with the police, who were alleged to believe that he also had something to do with Black's murder. The first approach used by Anderson was to try to get Mackerley to tell him about alleged past phone calls:

> *Anderson*: And he said that I said that your phone calls up to Black's telephone were after he disappeared. And I, and I said, "I don't believe I said that." And he said, "Yeah, that's what you said." And I don't remember what I read in the paper and what you told me, so I really don't know. I really don't. I don't know what I read 'cause I don't save any of the papers.

Mackerley: Well, what knowledge would you have of my phone calls?

Anderson: Well, 'cause you told me about erasing Black's phone recorder and all that shit.

Mackerley: But you didn't—

Anderson: [*interrupting*] I mean I have knowledge of your phone calls from you and, and what they're saying is that—

Mackerley: [*interrupting*] Where would, where would it come up that you would tell them that you had that?

Anderson: I don't know, Alan. The guy said that I said that the phone calls were after Black left New Jersey. Now I don't know if that means after he got down there and, and you did your thing or, or if it means after he was in flight. I'm not sure because I got the impression from you that you had made the phone calls after he was in the air.

Mackerley: Oh, and you told them—

Anderson: [*interrupting*] No, I didn't tell, I don't think I did, but this, I, I just want to know what you told me or what he said.

Mackerley: You would remember me saying something about making phone calls.

Anderson: Well, I know what you said. You said that you made the phone calls and everything. You had erased his recorder.

Mackerley: But, but you didn't tell them that.

Anderson: Fuck no. I didn't tell them that.

Mackerley: What I'm saying to you is I don't think you would ever have said that you had knowledge of me making phone calls.

Anderson: Well I don't think so either, okay?

Mackerley: Okay.

It's difficult to be certain about what this exchange proved. I cite it here primarily as an example of the retell strategy used by Anderson, in this case unsuccessful since its usefulness to the prosecution is tainted in the places where both of the men interrupted each other, by Anderson's contradictory statements that he told the police about what Mackerley had allegedly told him, and by Anderson's weak statement about the "impression" he got from his earlier conversation with Mackerley. Nor was Anderson's ambiguous, "you did your thing," explicit and strong enough to confirm that Mackerley, who appeared to ignore it anyway, was involved in the killing. Mackerley neither denied nor admitted the killing here, instead choosing to challenge what Anderson possibly could have known.

Switching from asking what Mackerley had told him, Anderson next modified this a bit by trying to get Mackerley to confirm what he was allegedly told:

> *Anderson*: Well you told me, you told me you went down and used the card in Miami.
> *Mackerley*: I would never have a fucking conversation and you know that I never had a conversation with anyone.
> *Anderson*: Okay.

Undaunted, Anderson tried the retell strategy again:

> *Anderson*: The other thing that they said that I said was wrong, this morning they said it. They said that I said that Lisa used a credit card.
> *Mackerley*: You said it or you read it in the paper?
> *Anderson*: Well see, that's what I don't know, see? And I don't know.
> *Mackerley*: That's in the paper.
> *Anderson*: Well, that's what I'm asking you. What's in the paper and what isn't?
> *Mackerley*: That's in the paper . . . Basically what you know about it is what you have read in the newspaper.

Again Anderson does not get anything incriminating out of Mackerley (if indeed, that information was actually in the newspaper). Anderson's retell strategy obviously did not elicit anything useful for the police so he moved on to another strategy: a request to be scripted in what he should tell the police the next time they interview him.

The Scripting Strategy

> *Anderson*: I wanted to make sure what it is so that I don't trip up. I got three choices. Leave the fucking country, go to jail with Lisa, and the other thing I'm gonna do is lie, okay.

Mackerley: I've never had a conversation with you about any of this.
Anderson: Alan! Have you told anybody that you told me?
Mackerley: Never . . . I never told anybody anything.
Anderson: And that's what I should say? You didn't tell anybody anything?
Mackerley: [inaudible]
Anderson: Look, what do you want me to do?
Mackerley: I don't know anything about [inaudible] so what the fuck can I answer?

Anderson played the role of a serious suspect in this case, one who might have to flee the country to avoid prosecution. Lisa Costello had gone to jail because she refused to talk about what she knew in the case, offering him a second option—to do the same thing. Anderson's third choice was to lie. Mackerley avoided responding to any of these choices, even after Anderson challenged him. Anderson's switch from the retell strategy to a request for Mackerley to script him about what to tell the police still yielded nothing useful. Mackerley's responses, though sometimes inaudible, triggered Anderson to challenge again, this time with false information fed him by his handlers:

The Lying Strategy

Anderson: Then why did she make that free remark to me that day or in front of me about the clerk couldn't have ID'd her when she, about the credit card or something. You remember, and I can, she left and I turned to you, I don't remember what she said but she left. Do you realize what that means?
Mackerley: That she wasn't there. . . . None of the above is factual because none of the above ever happened. I think the detective realized that when Lisa rented a rental car, they stamped a time and date on it and at some point in time, the police realized that Black's plane was in the air, if he was on it, the plane was in the air. So that all stopped.

Once again, the undercover strategy failed. Unbeknownst to Anderson, Mackerley already knew the facts that countered Anderson's attempt to use false information to get him to admit something incriminating.

The retell strategy is common and legitimate in undercover operations trying to recapture on tape the events that happened in the past. In fact, it often works very effectively for law enforcement. The scripting strategy is a bit more obvious and works less well on the whole. The lying strategy is dangerous, as Anderson learned in this case, especially if the target has adequate information to contradict it.

6

Interrupting, Overlapping, Lying, Not Taking "No" for an Answer, and Representing Illegality Differently to Separate Targets in a Stolen Property Case: *US v. Prakesh Patel and Daniel Houston*

Sometimes there is more than one target in an undercover tape operation. One of the targets may be inclined to reject the agent's suggestion to commit a criminal act while the other, usually a more susceptible target, is easier to ensnare. The stronger target may even say "no." When this happens, the prosecution is tempted to use the culpability of the weaker target to implicate the stronger one in the same criminal acts.

A case in 2002 brought by the DEA in the Western Judicial District of Oklahoma provides a good illustration of how this strategy can be used. After DEA agents had captured Ernie Titus, who admitted to being a methamphetamine manufacturer or "cook," they decided to use him as a cooperating witness to catch the retailers from whom Titus claimed to have obtained the large quantities of nasal decongestant containing pseudoephedrine (PSE) that he later used to manufacture and sell a controlled substance, meth. Titus told the DEA that he had previously purchased the decongestant at several local convenience stores and at a motel owned by Prakesh "Pete" Patel. He claimed that sometimes Patel would sell him case-load quantities of the nasal decongestant from his store and motel or that Patel would arrange for his clerk at one of his stores, Daniel Houston, to sell it to him.

Patel's defense attorney, Stephen Jones of Oklahoma City, sent me nine tape recordings that were made between May and August 2002. Cooperating witness Titus worked alone on the first seven tapes. The fact that the prosecution kept sending the cooperating witness back to get more conversation usually suggests that intelligence analysts considered the earlier tape recordings insufficient to make their case. This is a common problem when cooperating witnesses are given the task of capturing inculpatory evidence on tape. They are often unskilled in complying with legal requirements and their efforts often fall short or are otherwise flawed. When this happens, monitoring DEA agents may do follow-up undercover work themselves, either to obtain more conclusive evidence of the target's guilt or to suggest and capture on tape further illegal acts that expand the scope of the original operation.

It should be pointed out here that the case against Patel and Houston was very strong and that it is pretty clear that they indeed sold large quantities of products containing pseudoephedrine to Titus. But one of the legal guidelines is not very explicit, indicating that only small quantities, not amounts such as a case or more at a time, can be sold legally to retail customers. Patel was aware of the broad meaning of the guidelines, but he never seemed to understand what "small" and "large" quantities really meant.

Patel and Houston were ultimately found guilty at trial. Nevertheless, the following analysis shows how the cooperating witness and the agent used four important conversational strategies, including one that differentiated to each target the degree to which their act was illegal:

1. The investigators used very different representations of the illegality proposed; explicitly to Houston but vaguely to Patel.
2. The cooperating witness, Titus, blocked the target's understanding of his representation of illegality by uttering his inculpatory statements at the same time that the target was talking.
3. The agent camouflaged the illegality of the proposed purchase.
4. The agent refused to accept Patel's frequent efforts to say "no" to the scheme.

Using Different Representations of Illegality to Two Targets

As is noted in other chapters, the best representations of illegality are explicit ones. To the convenience store clerk, Daniel Houston, cooperating witness Titus used the words and expressions, "dope," "crank," and "sling some dope." At different times during the conversation he even asked Houston if he would like to make some money by becoming his "slinger":

> "You wouldn't know anybody'd want to sling a little dope for me, would you?"
> * * *
> "Did you . . . ever find somebody might wanna sling some for me?"
> * * *
> "Five hundred dollars if you find me a good slinger."
> * * *
> "I got me a girl to make some goddamn crank."
> * * *
> "I want to be able to come back down here with the dope and hand it to somebody and come back in a couple days for my money."
> * * *
> "But there's some serious money to be made, especially if you don't mess with it, you know what I'm sayin'?"

In contrast with such explicitness, the cooperating witness was much more ambiguous to Patel. Titus used expressions that were guarded and indirect. In his indirect references to what he does with the psuedoephedrine he wants to buy, Titus mentioned that he was planning to move to Kansas City to join forces with another man "who does what we do." In English, the dummy verb, "do," is used to stand in for an already identified antecedent. However, when such antecedent is never given, the listener is forced to infer what it means. It is possible that Patel could indeed infer Titus's real meaning, but the actual language Titus used is not explicit. Conclusive evidence in a criminal case rests more comfortably on clarity and explicitness rather than on the target's ability or willingness to guess at the meaning. The following shows examples of Titus's indirectness during his conversations with Patel, particularly with the dummy verb, "do":

> "See my buddy's up in Kansas City where I'm gonna *do* this at."
>
> * * *
>
> "I'm not in the habit of payin' money. I'm in the habit of makin' money."
>
> * * *
>
> "You know the difference between him and me? Is because he *does* what we *do* and he uses what we make."
>
> * * *
>
> "You can't be in this business that we *do* and be stupid."
>
> * * *
>
> ". . . and we've *done* this stuff together."

Rather than explicitly mentioning his intended use of the pheno, Titus assured Patel that it was "okay." Titus seemed to feel that it was not necessary to be clear and unambiguous. He even underlined this by claiming that Patel was actually aware of what he was "doing":

> "Your hands are stayin' clean. Obviously you know what we *do* with it . . . but we don't talk about it."

Did Patel "obviously know" this? The taped evidence does not make this clear. Titus seemed to justify his vague language by claiming, "we don't talk about it."

Toward the end of his conversations with Patel, the DEA agent took over the taping and, pretending to have been sent by Titus, tried to add a money laundering charge. He asked Patel what investments he might be able to make with all the money he'd been making. Note how the agent used the vague dummy noun here, "something," instead of an explicit one:

> *Agent*: What I'm doin' is kinda hard to explain, where that's comin' from, you know what I mean? If I could make a legitimate

investment. I might look at *doin' something* with you, invest in *somethin'* if you wanna show me some things and give me some legitimate—"

Blocking through Interruption and Overlapping

At one point during this topic about the agent's possible investments, Patel interrupted him and described a nearby hotel that was on the market and that he believed would be a good investment. Patel became quite animated about this topic, since hotels were the business that he knew a lot about. Following Patel's outline of various investment possibilities, the agent tried to be clear that he was really interested in finding a way to launder his money. The conversation, at this point, turned into a duel about who would hold the floor, and they were both talking at the same time when the agent tried to be more explicit about wanting Patel to help him launder his money, saying:

Titus	Patel
"But I'm just puttin' some money somewhere— (*Both start talking over each other.*) [—and cleaning it up and making it look like I have some legitimate stuff	[See he wanted 650 so you're lookin' (unintelligible twenty thousand dollars so you put down]
(*Separate turn-taking resumes.*)	as down payment and the rest the bank will give it, they're on a ten-year schedule. So a ten-year repayment is not bad.
Yeah. No, that wouldn't be too bad. [unintelligible] equity, not get [unintelligible] That's a good idea. . . . You're gonna be my financial adviser now.	

When people talk at the same time, the person with the loudest voice and, in this case, the one nearest to the mike, produces the clearest words that can be heard by later listeners to the tape. The government's transcript of their overlapping talk showed only the words of Titus, leaving Patel's words out altogether. Titus's voice was clear on the tape. Patel's was not. It often takes an experienced linguist using state-of-the-art equipment to crack the code of simultaneous speech. Could Patel have heard the agent's inculpatory words, "cleaning it up and making it look like I have some legitimate stuff"? Unless Patel was one of those rare individuals who can talk and listen at the same time, the agent's words about "cleaning up" the money were not likely to have been heard. But whether he heard it or not, the fact remains that simultaneous speech can only produce questionable evidence for the prosecution. In this case, the agent's overlapping blocked Patel's words and left the impression that the representation of illegality was clear. It clearly was not.

Camouflaging the Illegality

It is difficult to get into Patel's mind. He had indeed sold, or arranged to have sold, large quantities of decongestant containing pheno to Titus, even though he knew or strongly suspected that Titus used this product to cook meth. When, in the last two tape-recorded conversations in evidence, the agent approached Patel, claiming to have been sent to him by Titus so that he could buy the same pheno, Patel quickly explained that he didn't have any to sell. He was almost immediately agitated, warning the agent to stay away from Titus. He told the agent that in his last visit from Titus, another man had been with him and that this man had pulled out an identification card indicating he was "from the narcotics people." This somehow led Patel to think that Titus and the alleged narcotics man were working together on behalf of law enforcement and that they needed Patel's help in obtaining some pheno product to use in a sting to catch other meth cooks. Patel's mention of the man who displayed his narcotics identification apparently made the agent appear uncomfortable, leading Patel to warn the agent to not get caught in a drug sting:

Patel: You can't do stupid things.
Agent: No. And that's why I don't want to be around him.
Patel: I'm just going by the articles that I read in the paper you know, reading here.
Agent: Yeah, and I know, I mean your hands are staying clean.

In his previous statements concerning investing his money, note how the agent had made the claim that whatever he might invest in should be "legitimate." This triggered Patel's interest, since he considered himself very knowledgeable about the hotel business and its investment possibilities. They spent some fifteen minutes on this topic. Now Patel advised the agent to stay away from Titus and to not do anything stupid.

Throughout this conversation the agent continued his camouflage strategy, expressing the legitimacy of what the two of them are doing:

Agent: You know, there's nothing here. I mean, I don't do anything here I mean.
* * *
Agent: I mean your hands are staying clean.
* * *
Agent: So and then as long as you're okay, I guess we oughta do all right.

Ignoring the Target's Efforts to Say "No"

There are many ways to say "no." Some of them are direct and explicit, such as, "No, I won't get involved in something like that."

Most of the time, however, it seems difficult to say "no" to someone who requests something of us, largely because saying "no" can be face threatening, even impolite. We often fudge and try to find a more graceful way out. The following examples show some of the attempts made by Patel to reject the agent's requests.

In June, when the agent, posing as a purchaser, came to Patel claiming that cooperating witness Titus had told him that he could buy large quantities of pheno from Patel, Patel told him that he didn't know anything about such an arrangement and, furthermore, he didn't have any of the requested products on hand:

> *Patel*: I have a few convenience stores and that's the reason why I can get a few pills, because of the number of stores we have . . . we get a half a case anymore per store . . . but we can't get 'em anymore.
> *Agent*: Yeah, it seems to be gettin' tough and that's why.
> *Patel*: The FDA is controlling everything, which is fine. I mean, it don't matter. It's fine. We can make good money at it but the jail time is not worth it.
> *Agent*: No, no. It's you've got to be careful.
> *Patel*: For my protection, yes . . . and besides, we are all primarily hotel people. We have no desire to be a distributor on this pill thing, because I have a lot of people, they know me so they think, oh they come here, "Let me have some, let me." "Sorry, man." I mean the rest of the Patels, they have a good name here. I don't want to be accounted for spoiling the rest of their names here. Hell no.

At this point the agent did not accept this as a "no," and asked Patel to phone Titus, to verify that it's okay to sell him some pheno. Patel called Titus during his conversation with the agent and also told Titus that he didn't have any, concluding:

> *Patel*: I've told you before too, on this thing, that it's not, I'm not into this pill business. You've got to understand this . . . I've done my homework on this issue. I won't do anything because I have too much invested in real estate to even mess with this nonsense . . . I have people involved to just check what are the strict guidelines. And you have to know that 'cause there's nothing written in golden words that this is exactly what you can do on this aspect . . . I've had my attorney check . . . and he said there is no set rule but they ask you to use your common sense. Why would somebody want to buy twelve cases of nasal congestant? . . . and the other thing is that if you know the intentions of what people are going to make out of it then it's a legit sell and those things can put you in trouble but not for, say, just selling six dozens will put somebody in trouble.

Undaunted by Patel's roundabout, indirect, or even incompetent way of saying "no" here, the agent persisted:

> Agent: My only thing is that I have to go back up to Kansas City . . . it's ridiculous how much they want for it up there. I had a guy that would off the truck give it to me —
> Patel: A lot of people get caught, man.
> Agent: —and it's not worth me drivin' all the way back up there, especially when he told me I could come here and he said two thousand for a case.

Possibly because of the mention of two thousand a case, Patel's resolve began to fade. He pointed out that he had warned Titus about the dangers of his getting caught and had told him that he didn't want him to come around anymore. He even warned the agent to stay away from Titus. Patel then asked for the agent's phone number and promised to call him back, adding: "If I have it, just swing by here . . . it's not a problem."

Two months later, unannounced, the agent swung by Patel's motel with money for six cases. Patel said, "That's fair." Curiously, having agreed to sell the decongestant containing pheno to the agent, Patel continued to say that he would no longer sell it to Titus.

> Patel: I'm just saying "no." And then he (Titus) called me and I said, "Ernie, let's draw a line man, because I gave you a few cases, you can't change any [unintelligible] . . . Because this is not what I live off. I don't need to do this. Bottom line, this is something we get it, so I mean I don't even need to carry it.
> Agent: It's some nice extra money.
> Patel: It is. But it's not worth it to go in there for twenty-five years and have a bad name for us in my community . . . I'm not for that. Shit, hell with that damn thing . . . you see it's not worth it . . . I won't do that. I don't want to be a part of that.

The case against Patel was strong. Even though he said "no" to both Titus and the agent, Patel illegally sold large quantities of the product anyway, making his "no" responses hollow in the eyes of the law. Patel seemed to be torn between saying that he did not want to do anything illegal and doing that very same thing anyway. I still wonder what Patel was really thinking by his sometimes contradictory statements to Titus and the DEA agent. I am reminded again of the Abscam case of Florida Congressman Richard Kelly, who said "no" to an offer of a bribe eight times on tape, then, with the videotape rolling, stood up and stuffed twenty-five thousand dollars in bribe money into his pockets. (See chapter 2.) The Kelly and Patel cases had one thing in common: they both claimed to be trying to be on the side of the law when they committed their illegal acts. Obviously, this is not a very successful defense theory.

In Patel's case the undercover operation succeeded and the four strategies used here seem to have been helpful toward showing his guilt. Nevertheless, the use of these strategies also provides examples of how law enforcement can use them to help enhance the appearance of criminality when the target at least sometimes struggled to keep his nose clean.

7

Eleven Little Ambiguities and How They Grew in a Business Fraud Case: US v. Paul Webster and Joe Martino

Just before the end of the twentieth century, members of several different crime families learned that they were about to be indicted for promoting a large-scale racketeering operation that was alleged to be unlawfully engaged in interstate and foreign commerce. In an effort to avoid being charged, these crime families allegedly decided to work together to identify informants and potential cooperating witnesses that they believed had assisted the FBI in its investigations and who had agreed to testify in federal criminal trials against their fellow members. Their reason for "identifying" such people is fairly obvious in the world of crime families.

Before such identification could happen, however, one of those netted in this FBI operation already had agreed to be a cooperating witnesses, to pose as a stock investor, and to secretly tape-record a series of conversations with certain stock brokers that they claimed were in on the conspiracy. These conversations comprised the evidence against the two brokers whose case is described in this chapter. At the request of their attorneys, all names are changed in this account. We will call the two stockbroker defendants in this case Paul Webster and Joe Martino. The cooperating witness, who met with the stock brokers over a six-month period, will be called Al Cicotte. The defendant's lawyers will not be named.

The scenario used by the cooperating witness and two undercover FBI agents was to make it appear that they had investors ready to purchase stocks that the targets had been brokering. Cicotte was the perfect person for the government to use in this sting since the agents were not nearly as well versed in how to carry out this charade. The targets ran a corporation with complex stock operations involving stocks that the corporation owned while, at the same time, also serving as brokers for many stocks that they did not own or control themselves. Martino worked for Webster, the ultimate decision maker, who actually appears on very few of the tapes. It was Martino's main job to meet potential clients to raise money.

The major portion of the investment conversations concerned a union's pension fund. Cicotte tried to arrange a deal whereby this union would purchase stocks from one of Martino's funds. After several weeks of discussion about this deal, Cicotte began to hint that a kickback to certain union representatives would be needed in order to jump-start the process. The criminal legal issues centered on whether or not Cicotte and the agents were clear and unambiguous about their bribery kickback suggestion, whether Martino and Webster actually agreed to it, and the extent to which any transaction was consummated. The purpose of this analysis is not to describe the entire case but, rather, to show how Cicotte's conversational strategy of ambiguity was used throughout the tapes as he tried to make commonly used words and expressions appear to be covert and illegal. This chapter describes Cicotte's use of eleven such terms and expressions.

Following the common undercover strategy of starting with a scenario that is completely legal, with only hints of possible illegality, Cicotte's exchanges used the following expressions throughout his conversation:

1. "Quietly" and "Friendly"

". . . and the objective is *to do this very quietly* . . . with a minimum if any of fanfare."

* * *

"There's a group of fund managers who I'm *friendly* with on a personal level . . ."

* * *

"The guys buying this *are extremely friendly* . . . *will do it quietly*."

In the stock market it is not unusual to make moves "quietly" in order to avoid attracting the attention of others who might want in on a good thing. Nor has it ever been considered illegal to do business with "friendly" people. These expressions, found in their early conversations, may be considered hints of something more to come but they cannot in themselves be strong enough evidence to indicate that a representation of illegality had taken place. In order to have alerted the targets to an illegal intent, more explicit terms, such as "secretly" and "hidden" might have replaced the ambiguous "quietly" here. Something a bit closer to the idea of "co-conspirators" might have replaced "friendly."

2. "Clean It Up"

>*(after Webster had described how interest had paid dividends and that sometimes he had margins with clients who then asked him to move it to other investments)*
>"Yeah, they want you to *clean it up* or whatever."
>* * *
>*(after Webster had explained that his practice was to preserve the price of stock by buying it)*
>"Well, you *cleaned up* everything and . . ."

We "clean up" things by making them tidy, better organized, or corrected in some way. The expression, "clean it up," also has some relevance in the context of money laundering, but is benign in the context of moving stock to different places at the request of customers or preserving the price by buying it up. Cicotte was clearly trying to make the tape look inculpatory, but his suggestion is so removed from the current context that Webster didn't even catch the hint.

3. "Credibility"

>"This deal was originally sent to me from a group that I would consider to be having almost negative *credibility* . . . zero *credibility*."
>* * *

"It's peculiar because that deal was basically shown to me from two sources which I don't consider to be *credible*."

Cicotte claimed that he got the idea for the transaction he was now proposing to Webster and Martino from a source that was questionable in its qualifications. Following one dictionary definition, "credible" means "the quality or power of inspiring belief." Even saying that the source was not credible, of course, is a step away from saying that the deal itself was not credible.

Cicotte later claimed that he had figured out ways to make that noncredible source's idea work better, trying to associate "credible" with them rather than the source. Following another dictionary definition of "credibility," it means, "the offer of reasonable grounds for being believed." Cicotte shifted the meaning to the credibility that they could have by using the plan:

> "Okay, and, and it seems to me that that gives us tremendous availability of cash, insofar as margin. It gives us tremendous, quote, *credibility*."

It is difficult to understand how the word, "credibility," might be considered a representation of illegality by Cicotte, but this was the hint that he was apparently trying to make here. Putting verbal quotes around the word was another attempt to do this, but it, like the rest of his effort, failed to make explicit the idea that this deal was not legal or, for that matter, credible.

4. "Profit Sharing"

Cicotte's major undercover task was to indicate somehow to Webster and Martino that a kickback or bribe would be necessary in order for them to get the union to purchase their stocks. He avoided these words throughout the many taped conversations, choosing more indirect terms instead. One such attempt was with the words, "profit sharing."

> "Although you'll never see this, there's going to be some, some *profit sharing*."

The accepted meaning of "profit sharing" is a system or process through which employees receive a part of the profits of an industrial or commercial enterprise. In itself, this practice is common today, and it in no way denotes anything illegal. If Cicotte wanted to be clear here, he could have said "kickback" or "bribe," which would have been a more accurate representation of what he apparently meant.

5. "Putting It Away"

> "The only way *I'm putting this thing away* is through my relationship with the boys who are *putting it away*."
>
> * * *
>
> "How would you expect we ameliorate those particular issues by *putting the stuff away*? I mean we can't *put it away* for seven percent."
>
> * * *
>
> "Stock runs back up over a period of three or four months to ten bucks, I could be *putting that stuff away* all day long."

The various meanings of "put away" are primarily negative: to discard, divorce, renounce, bury, and kill are the most obvious, with the only possibly positive meanings, to consume or save. By using "put away" instead of the more commonly used business terms, such as buy, sell, broker, or complete a deal, Cicotte cleverly tried to add a negative tone to an everyday stock transaction without actually saying anything illegal.

6. "Quid Pro Quo"

> "I'm putting this thing away through my relationship and my *quid pro quo* with the boys who are putting it away."
>
> * * *
>
> (*after Martino had just explained that it's easier and a lot faster to sign an escrow statement to the bank*):
> "Yeah, but the *quid pro quo* arrangement was going to be done simultaneously anyway under the old plan."
>
> * * *

"You have to go over certain things. My input on the document is *quid pro quo*, which is only as good as the guy behind it."

"Quid pro quo" is a Latin term that means, simply, something for something else. It is sometimes used in business transactions relating to the sale of something for a price. Lately it also has been associated with a bribe or a kickback, although this is clearly not its only meaning. By using it here, Cicotte appears to be trying to associate his part of the potential transaction with something illegal. Interestingly, Webster and Martino paid no attention and did not respond to Cicotte's words. At that point their total attention was on busily calculating the percentages being discussed about the transaction and they went right on doing so.

7. "Crafty"

> *Cicotte*: I mean it sounded quite, quite, uh, quite *crafty* that you were going to issue in some fashion First Washington Financial.
> *Martino*: Maybe that would be the easiest way to do it because you wouldn't even have to make the sales.

The adjective, "crafty," carries both positive and negative denotations. The positive sense is skill in planning, making, or executing; a type of dexterity. The negative sense is skill or guile in deceiving to gain an end. That Martino interpreted only the positive meaning is evidenced by his above response, which indicated an efficient method rather than a deceptive one.

8. "Hiccup"

Cicotte had dealt mostly with Martino, so when he finally got a chance to meet with Martino's boss, Webster, he concocted a plan to rope him into what he was trying to hint about to Martino—that there would be an illegal kickback to the union representatives. Cicotte's plan was first to suggest that Martino was thinking of retiring soon, leaving them with nobody who would know the important and allegedly covert details of the deal. Cicotte refers to such an event as a "hiccup":

"If we put the German insurance company in for twenty million then some of the other unions which will follow suit go in and we're up to fifty or sixty million, okay? And there's some kind of *hiccup* here and Joe Martino's not there, you're gonna say, "Well fuckin' Joe, you know, blah, blah, blah, you know."

* * *

"There's no question he's extremely bright so the issue here is, you know, he's not there in six months and there's a *hiccup*, okay?"

* * *

"Well I don't want it to be, and *hiccups* are *hiccups*, but, you know, I'll get into this a little later."

* * *

Cicotte: We need to make sure that there's no *hiccup* with this instrument.
Webster: Well, they're preferred stock.

Cicotte's choice of "hiccup" was clever, for he ambiguously used the word to hint that it might refer to some kind of discovery about the allegedly illegal matters that he and Martino had been discussing earlier. Cicotte's apparent hope was that "hiccup" would also suggest that Webster might not honor the supposed spoken agreement to pay the kickback that Cicotte was alleged to have had in his discussions with Martino.

However, Webster did not interpret Cicotte's intention in this way. Instead, he missed any hint of illegality as his responded that they were discussing preferred stock, which was not likely to "hiccup." Webster had adopted Cicotte's use of "hiccup" in a totally economic sense, unrelated to Martino's alleged plan to retire and to do anything illegal. Cicotte, now caught in his own metaphor, finally gave up and adopted Webster's meaning of "hiccup" as an economic downturn:

"But if we get into an economic downturn and whatever, you guys have to look me in the eye and assure me that, at least for a period of time, we're not gonna have a *hiccup* with this . . . What I'm concerned with is that in a compressed period of time, if we have a little bit of economic shock and the debt markets dry up . . . "

Cicotte's effort to use a benign word, such as "hiccup," failed completely here. He did not succeed in drawing Webster into anything and he had failed to establish that any previous oral covert illegal agreement with Martino had ever existed.

9. "Involved"

In over several months of discussion with Cicotte, Webster and Martino tried to turn his attention to several other more promising transactions, but Cicotte's effort to make their deals look illegal continued just the same. Since a great deal depended on his ability to net more targets for the prosecution, Cicotte kept coming back with new scenarios, potential purchasers, and reasons for delays. Finally it became apparent that Webster and Martino were beginning to suspect that Cicotte was not above board in his morals and schemes. At one point, late in the investigation, Webster and Martino met with Cicotte saying the following:

> *Webster*: We're not *involved* in anything where any fees are going back to any union or anything like that.
> *Martino*: Right.
> *Cicotte*: Did I *involve* you in that?
> *Webster*: Nope. I don't know anything about union internal fees. I don't want to know anything about fees.
> *Martino*: I don't either.
> *Cicotte*: Did I tell you?
> *Webster*: What? About—
> *Cicotte*: (*interrupting*) I wouldn't say you wanted it. Why would you want to know?
> *Webster*: I don't.
> *Cicotte*: I have a better one. I wouldn't want you to know.
> *Webster*: I don't know anything. Don't wanna know.

Here Webster clearly said that they were not involved, conventionally meaning that they were not obliged to take part or occupy themselves absorbingly or commit or occupy themselves to be included or enveloped in it (see any dictionary definition of "involve" here). Nor were they a necessary accompaniment to such a plan. In short, Webster said clearly that they were not involved.

Apparently Cicotte's hints had failed once more. But in this passage, Cicotte quickly concocted another strategy, a very clever tactic, asking, "Did I *involve* you in that?" If Webster had answered that Cicotte certainly tried to involve them in that, Cicotte may have gotten the evidence on tape that Webster and Martino at least knew about the kickback scheme. But Webster's "nope" denied that they were involved. They certainly suspected something was haywire by this time but they believed that they had successfully distanced themselves from it.

The challenge of this meeting was a turning point for Cicotte. He was about to lose his prey, but he still had one more ambiguous trick up his sleeve. Building on Webster's "I don't want to know anything about fees," Cicotte countered, "Why would you wanna know?" followed by "I wouldn't want you to know." This turned out to be one of the strong arguments used by the prosecution to show the guilt of Webster and Martino. Cicotte managed to give the impression that the two men were perfectly willing to go along with the kickback scheme as long as they were not told explicitly what was going on. Cicotte did not say, "There's nothing for you to know." Instead, his "I wouldn't want you to know" appeared to verify that he was being careful with his words to them as they together carried out the kickback scheme. Such an interpretation was thought to nullify Websters earlier denial, "We're not involved in anything where any fees are going back to any union or anything like that." Cicotte had now made Websters denial look like only an effort to appear innocent.

Webster was bested here. He apparently didn't catch the significance of Cicotte's clever language construction. Cicotte did not explicitly admit that he himself was involved in a kickback. Instead, he uttered a hypothetical statement about what he would want if it were the case that he was engaged in such behavior. But the damage was done anyway. The allusion had been made. Cicotte was hinting, for the benefit of later listeners to the tape, that Webster and Martino were being coy with language, trying to deny that they "knew" about the kickback scheme even though they had actually known about it.

If Cicotte had wanted to be clear and unambiguous here, it would not have been difficult. He could have said forthrightly that he was indeed involved in a kickback and that they should have inferred as much from what he had hinted to them previously. But that probably wouldn't have succeeded nearly as well as his plan to make a tape in which the jurors could infer that Webster and Martino had inferred this from the beginning.

10. "Exposure"

This noun has primarily honorable senses, centering on the subject's becoming widely well-known, being protected from harm, being subject to some external effect or influence, and being put at risk from outside harmful elements. It also has one less-than-honorable meaning: having something secret or covert disclosed to the public.

Cicotte was apparently mindful of the possible dishonorable meaning of "exposure" in his following exchange with Webster. Webster had just explained that the fund goes to First Washington Financial, which has 18% discounts and commissions. Webster then consulted with Martino, asking him where it should go from there. Martino replied that he hadn't broken it all down yet. Then Webster explained:

> *Webster:* I just don't know what's on it. We would have to make sure we don't get any *exposure* as to who gets this 18 percent.
> *Cicotte:* I don't want any *exposure* either. So what's your definition of *exposure?*
> *Martino:* It's going to First Washington Financial.
> *Cicotte:* We want this to be somewhat quiet, secretive, if you will.

Cicotte cleverly latched onto Webster's noun, "exposure," and tried to determine whether or not Webster had the secretive, covert meaning in mind. Since Cicotte's question was ignored, he got nothing supportive, so he elaborated and redefined "exposure" as "quiet" and "secretive." Neither Webster nor Martino appeared to catch the significance of Cicotte's effort to make the transaction look illegal. Nevertheless, from this point on, Cicotte dropped his attempt at defining "exposure" as covert:

> (*speaking about a possible deal with a German insurance company*)

"So if they're gonna hold the mortgage directly, which I don't think they would do, I don't think they're gonna want to, I don't know their limitation of *exposure* in one particular item."

This time Cicotte used "exposure" to mean putting all their financial eggs in one basket, a kind of investment placement strategy that is known to be risky. There was no hint of illegality in this. He did the same in the following conversation:

"They tend to not have maximum *exposure* in lending or investment capacity for more than one hundred million."

Cicotte first used "exposure" in an attempt to color the dealings he was having with Webster and Martino. And once again they didn't bite and so he gave up and finally adopted the meaning that they had in mind rather than anything untoward. In a sense, this constitutes both the contamination strategy and the hit-and-run strategy. He contaminated the tape with the word, "secretive," and used the hit-and-run strategy by first hinting at illegality, then returning to the word's standard business usage. His effort was not exactly successful, but it didn't make any difference because the illusion of illegality was put on tape.

11. "Beyond the Norm"

Cicotte: (*continuing to discuss the deal with a German insurancecompany*) And they're quite capable of doing one-off transactions. You know, something, something *beyond the norm* that is a little complex. So that's something that they can be utilized if you have something in mind.
Webster: Well, would they do a real-estate loan?

"Beyond the norm" means simply something unusual or different from what is expected or normal. Cicotte continued to be indirect and cautious in his effort to represent illegality, using still another ambiguous expression in the hope that Webster would self-generate something to indicate his willingness to stretch the law. That Webster did not catch the drift of "beyond the norm" can be seen in his follow-up question about doing a real-estate loan, which was not beyond the norm for an insurance company to do. Cicotte's next response was, "This is something I gotta think about 'cause it's off the norm for us." The expression was then dropped.

Who Wins and Who Loses?

In a linguistic sense, all of these examples of how Cicotte, the cooperating witness, used common expressions to try to make it appear that a crime was being committed may be said to have failed badly. In each case, Webster and Martino either didn't catch the hints that Cicotte put forth or they adopted only their noninculpatory meanings. Cicotte's most successful effort was with his use of "involved," where, in spite of Webster's denial of involvement, Cicotte cleverly played to any future listeners to the tape recordings, encouraging them to infer that Webster and Martino could have inferred that a kickback was being made. The danger of inferential meaning was doubled here.

Despite my analyses of these eleven efforts (I was not called on to testify), the defense attorneys apparently did not manage to use them effectively at trial. Cicotte's ambiguous uses of expressions that created the illusions of guilt were apparently all the jury needed (or wanted). Webster and Martino were found guilty just the same.

8

Discourse Ambiguity in a Contract Fraud Case: *US v. David Smith*

In 1997 federal prosecutors brought a criminal conspiracy case against David Smith, the president of a Texas manufacturer of helicopters. Like many such cases, the issues were very complex. Smith's company, a subsidiary of a French manufacturer, had obtained a contract to produce a number of military-type helicopters for the nation of Israel. Since Israel is regarded as an ally of the United States, this transaction was eligible for the U.S. Foreign Military Financing Program (FMF), which was created to promote the interests of domestic American businesses by providing U.S. funds to allies to help pay for the costs of such manufacture. As long as the helicopters were manufactured in the United States, FMF could support a large percentage of Israel's costs. If only some parts of the helicopters were manufactured in the United States, only a proportional amount of the purchase was eligible for FMF support. In addition, FMF was not limited to military equipment but also could be applied to the manufacture and sale of other hardware and equipment produced in the United States and then sold to allies.

For unclear reasons, the U.S. government suspected that Smith's company had been falsely documenting the amount of FMF money to which Israel was entitled. Rather than starting at the top with Smith, the FBI agents went after Smith's employee, Ron Tolfa, who was in charge of the company's contract with Israel. They convinced Tolfa that something illegal was going on and got his cooperation to wear a hidden mike and tape-record four conversations with his boss, David Smith. These tapes, beginning in April 1995 and ending in July 1996, constituted the major evidence compiled against Smith. They were sent to me for linguistic analysis by his defense attorney, Mark Werbner of Dallas.

It was possible that the French parent company may have had some knowledge or involvement in this matter but the case against Smith centered on whether or not he and his subsidiary company had such knowledge and involvement. As is usual in such cases, the issue was not only whether or not Smith and his company knew about the alleged false documentation but also whether they "should have known" about such things.

Tolfa's assignment was to elicit on tape Smith's alleged knowledge of it. The scenario created by the government was for Tolfa to report to Smith that government investigators had begun to look carefully at their contract. The four conversations in which Tolfa and Smith were alone together were tape-recorded but did not produce any clear and convincing evidence that Smith had knowledge of any false documentation. Nevertheless, the government officials cited certain passages of these conversations that, in their opinion, suggested Smith's complicity and knowledge of the French parent company's complicity. Based on these passages, Smith was indicted and tried.

It is not uncommon in such transactions to have an outside broker carry on much of the business. The prosecution alleged that the outside broker in this case, Ori Edelsburg, was illegally paid with FMF funds. If this were true, and if Smith knew or "should have known" this, it would prove that Smith was indeed involved in the alleged conspiracy to defraud. On the other hand, if Edelsburg was receiving his commission from the French parent company on some other aspect of the complex transaction not involving FMF funding, no criminal case could be made against Smith.

Not surprisingly, broker Edelsburg had put together a very complex, two-part transaction that included not only the sale of new helicopters produced by Smith's company to be sold to Israel but also the sale of certain older, used equipment to be sold by Israel to Chile. The latter part of the deal was between Edelsburg and the Israeli government and it was outside the boundary of FMF support. It was entirely proper for him to receive a commission for this part of the deal. Confusion about where Edelsburg's commission came from was at the center of the trial.

Tolfa did his best to elicit Smith's knowledge of any commission that Edelsburg might receive, but he failed to disambiguate what this commission was actually for. Smith's responses to Tolfa's somewhat vague hints and suggestions were at first commonly made with the feedback marker "uh-huh," then with expressions of surprise, and finally with outright denials that the broker ever got any commission related to FMF moneys. Aided by my analysis of Smith's responses to Tolfa's suggestions of illegality, Smith's attorney, Mark Werbner, was able to obtain an acquittal of Smith on all charges.

Tolfa was well coached in his efforts. He carefully followed the standard pattern of first trying to elicit Smith's self-generated guilt. When this failed, Tolfa went on to step two, throwing out hints that a guilty person might understand, a procedure that might be called "fishing." In fairness to this stage of undercover work, it should be noted that such hints are, by definition, planned and structured ambiguously, and their use at this stage might not be considered an unfair sting tactic. Examples of Tolfa's structured ambiguity include the following throughout the four tapes made when the two men were alone together:

April 1995

>*Tolfa*: Ori's calling me every day . . . he's worried, I guess, about his payment, his commission.
>*Smith*: Uh-huh.

Notice here that Tolfa has not said "commission paid by our company." Nor has he specified where any such commission is from. Smith, knowing that brokers get commissions, does not appear to be bothered by what Tolfa suggests, since he is aware that Edelsburg can get a legitimate commission on the other part of the transaction that dealt with the sale of the second-hand equipment going from Israel to Chile as well as commissions from his own company that did not relate to FMF-funded projects.

May 1995

>*Tolfa*: Ori's been beatin' me over the head about this payment. He thinks you're stupid.

Smith: [*laughs*]
Tolfa: He wants his commission.
Smith: So he gets paid when we get paid, huh? Is that how it works?
Tolfa: He's pounding on me every time there's a payment due.
Smith: What, is he panicking a little bit now for some reason?

Here Smith reveals his lack of familiarity about how the process works, asking his more knowledgeable contract manager as much. The closest this passage comes to implicating Smith is when Tolfa says Edelsburg "is pounding" on him when, if the commission is for the Chilean part of the deal, he should be pounding on the French parent company. But even if Edelsburg was to get a commission from Smith's company, there is nothing in this exchange to indicate that it would be paid from the FMF part of the contract. Tolfa's "every time there's a payment due" relates to the fact that payment in such transactions is based on the company's meeting various milestones in the production of the helicopters.

October 1995

Tolfa: ECF [the French parent company] has, you know, Ori's contract.
Smith: Uh-huh.
Tolfa: If they [investigators] get their hands on that, then we have a problem with the certification.
Smith: We didn't want the same signature on the cert as on the main. That was check and balance.
Tolfa: If they (investigators) can get ECF's (the French parent company's) documentation and find out that Ori's getting a commission—
Smith: (*interrupting before Tolfa can say what commission he is talking about*) AEC [Smith's company] did not have one on this contract. ECF (the French parent company) will tie this to Ori on the Chile transaction.

Tolfa continued his structured ambiguity, hoping to elicit Smith's knowledge of something illegal. The "certification" he spoke of is a required letter from Smith's company documenting the process. That Smith didn't catch Tolfa's ambiguous meaning here is evidenced by his response, in which Smith opined that the problem stemmed from the fact that he (Smith) signed the main contract but that another company official had signed the certification about FMF entitlements to the Israeli government. This wasn't what Tolfa was getting at so he quickly corrected this, saying that it would be a problem for them if the investigators got hold of the French parent company's documentation showing that Edelsburg would get a commission. Even though Tolfa hinted that the parent company's documentation may show that Ori would get a commission, he did not specify which part of which transaction involved the commission. Smith then interrupted and assured Tolfa that he was sure that any commission paid by the French parent company was related to the part of the transaction that dealt with Israel's sale of used equipment to Chile, which would be perfectly proper as long as it was separate from FMF funds which Smith apparently believed it was.

After over a year of not being successful at eliciting anything inculpatory from Smith, the government made another attempt, this time apparently instructing Tolfa to abandon indirectness and hints and to go for the gold by asking Smith point-blank about Edelsburg's involvement.

July 1996

> *Tolfa*: How does Ori get involved in this?
> *Smith*: Ori's gonna have to be paid through EFC (the French parent company) you know, outbound loop.

Here Tolfa was more direct than in the past, asking outright about Edelsburg's involvement. If ever there was an opportunity for Smith to implicate his own company, it was now. He responded that any payment would have to come from the parent company, but Smith did not say whether or not such payment was to be paid out of FMF moneys. Why not? Possibly because he considered this obvious and clear to Tolfa in the first place. People often do not elaborate on the obvious, especially when they see no particular reason to make this clear to the person who, as manager of the whole transaction, ought to know it.

So Tolfa's hinting stage in his conversations with Smith still yielded no clear and unambiguous evidence of Smith's involvement. The government then sent Tolfa back once more to make still another tape, this one involving Tolfa, Smith, and two high-level executives representing the French parent company, Patrick Rudloff and Regis Pierquat. In this conversation the speakers clearly represent their own understanding of the FMF requirements:

> *Rudloff*: According to the maximum payment of the customers, we are going to see if we are meeting production on the final price, which we don't know exactly, so, the gray area is FMF or not FMF at the present time. We don't know, he said maybe, maybe not. It's according to their budget. I think where the money's coming from is the trading of the two helicopters [the Israel to Chile transaction]. We have dropped the budget outside of FMF. Our company's opinion is to avoid FMF as much as possible because it's making a lot of problems for us here for the transfer price.
>
> *Smith*: Patrick, if they go FMF, what parts of that would be eligible for FMF?
>
> *Rudloff*: I am not sure.
>
> *Tolfa*: Well, the FMF funding will cover whatever is the U.S. content.
>
> *Smith*: Of course. You know the AEC 8.2 will be eligible, because of American man-hours in the assembly and completion. How do we figure that part of the EFC (the French parent company) was eligible for FMF?
>
> *Pierquat*: Nothing.
>
> *Smith*: Yeah, that's right.
>
> *Pierquat*: In the basic aircraft there is almost nothing eligible for FMF. It's just too complicated ... So I decided, in a best case, you would have 32 percent non-FMF. Either take all the spares, U.S. spares, and ferret out whatever.
>
> *Smith*: Um-hmm.
>
> *Pierquat*: The highest U.S. content would be 68 percent.

Here it is very clear that Smith is wondering what part of the contract is eligible for FMF, evidence that he knows that he can get FMF for only the parts that are made in the United States. Pierquat supports him in this, following precisely what the law says.

As an undercover elicitation strategy, ambiguity can be a very effective tool for uncovering a crime in the initial stages of an inquiry. The less explicit an undercover agent is, the greater is the opportunity for targets to clarify that ambiguity and possibly to implicate themselves in the process. When this happens, the investigators have done their work well. But what does it mean when the targets do not clarify the ambiguities, and thereby appear to implicate themselves? There are four possibilities:

1. The targets may understand the drift of the ambiguity and may be indeed guilty.
2. The targets' attention may be on something else and they simply miss the hint.
3. The targets may be so afraid to talk about the issue that they retreat into silence, or even suspect that they are being tape-recorded.
4. The targets are so innocent that they do not even catch the drift of the hinted ambiguity or innuendo.

These were the major passages of the tapes upon which the prosecution based its case against Smith and his company. Tolfa's conversational strategy of ambiguous representations of potential illegality did not yield incriminating responses, but they gave the illusion, to the prosecution at least, that a crime had indeed been committed, largely because Smith did not apparently make it clear enough for them to believe that he did not want to violate any FMF regulations. It is difficult to understand why an accused target needs to say repeatedly that he wants to follow the law. In this case the prosecution was based on the absence of Smith's saying he wanted to be legal, something that never occurred to him as even being necessary. Smith's responses to Tolfa's suggestions fall clearly into category four above—he never caught the hints.

Based on these undercover tapes, it seems difficult to understand why this case went to trial at all, especially after the effort led to rather clear indications that Smith's company was trying hard to determine exactly which parts of the manufacturing process were eligible for FMF and which were not. One cannot fault the government's use of the ambiguity strategy. What it lacked was an effective intelligence analysis that would have revealed the hopelessness of their case before time, money, reputation, and the suspect's emotional state of mind were unnecessarily spent. At trial, when Tolfa's conversational strategy of ambiguity was finally revealed, and Smith's responses were contextualized, the case against Smith evaporated and he was acquitted.

9

Contamination and Manipulation in a Bribery Case: US v. Paul Manziel

In early 2002 the FBI conducted a sting operation targeting Bobby Joe Manziel, a businessman in Tyler, Texas. The Manziel family owned several businesses in the city, where they were all considered prominent, if politically controversial, citizens. The FBI used handyman Eddie Williams, a local acquaintance of Manziel, as a cooperating witness. Williams had been arrested for various crimes and he agreed to wear a mike and try to get incriminating information from Bobby Joe Manziel. Williams spent two months doing this, at times tape-recording the entire Manziel family, but focusing his effort on Bobby Joe Manziel, who was thought to be willing to engage in some kind of criminal activity if given the chance. During his taping, Williams single-handedly created an alleged bribery scheme involving Bobby Joe Manziel's younger brother, Paul Manziel, and so he also taped several conversations that led to Paul's indictment on charges of bribery.

Some months earlier, in order to avoid the nuisance of a trial, Paul Manziel had pleaded guilty to a highly questionable drunken-driving charge and was serving his sentence of community service by teaching business courses five days a week at a local business school. The new bribery charge grew out of discussions about how Paul could speed up the completion of his community service hours by doing additional service at PATH (People Attempting to Help), a local nonprofit organization set up to help the needy in the Tyler area. This idea was suggested by Williams, who knew the man at PATH who was in charge of arranging for such work, Lorenzo Steward. Steward also repaired air conditioners on the side and, knowing that Bobby Joe had properties needing air conditioner repairs, Williams used this as an excuse to set up a meeting between Steward and Bobby Joe. During this meeting, Williams suggested to Bobby Joe and Steward that Paul might be able to work off some of his community service at PATH. Bobby Joe liked the idea and arranged for Williams to give Steward one hundred dollars cash, which the government claimed was a bribe for Steward to cook the books to make it appear that Paul would get credit for work that he wouldn't really do. In sharp contrast, Bobby Joe claimed that this money was an advance on air conditioner repairs that Steward would be doing for him.

From the beginning it was clear that Paul was never told about the one hundred dollars. To satisfy the police in his role as a secret, undercover, cooperating witness, Williams's tasks were:

1. to get Bobby Joe to invest two thousand dollars in a drug scheme that Williams knew about from personal experience;
2. to get Paul to show that he knew about the one hundred dollars that his brother Bobby Joe gave to Steward and to show that Paul agreed to cheat on reporting his community-service hours.

The FBI had given Williams the tape-recording equipment for a total of ten days during the months of April and May. Since Paul was not the original target of the sting operation, he was not recorded on most of these tapes. In fact, his relevant participation can be heard on only the last two. During the ten days that he had the recording equipment, Williams was not closely monitored, and he was given the freedom to turn his tape recorder off and on whenever he wanted to do so, at times resulting in a mishmash of seemingly disconnected talk, along with long periods of static, walking, and traffic sounds. This produced evidence that was usually of very low-quality audibility. For example, on the first tape, containing conversations between Williams and Bobby Joe, the government's own transcript marked 730 places that were deemed inaudible. Even the casual listener to the tapes could tell that Williams turned the tape off and on at will, sometimes in the middle of an ongoing conversation.

To complicate things further, when the prosecution gave the taped evidence to the defense to fulfill its discovery requirement, it was found that there were seven other tapes that, suspiciously enough, contained no audible conversations at all. As noted in chapter 2, when on/off signatures occur on tapes, one can never know what exculpatory evidence might have been excluded by the person doing the taping. When there is nothing at all on the tapes, suspicion mounts. Williams also took advantage of the fact that throughout the tapes, various people, including the targets, Bobby Joe and Paul, kept arriving and leaving. This led to crucial things being said on tape when the Manziels were not even present to participate in the conversations.

Soon after his indictment, Paul Manziel's defense attorneys, Cynthia Orr and Gerald Goldstein of San Antonio, sent me the tapes to analyze linguistically. The only evidence in the case against Bobby Joe consisted of five very long tape recordings made in late April and May. In the third of these, Bobby Joe agreed to invest two thousand dollars in a quick-money drug scheme suggested by Williams, providing the evidence needed to indict him. At that point, Williams turned his attention to brother Paul, who was in no way suspected of drug trafficking. Williams's first step was to suggest to Bobby Joe (still uncharged) that an acquaintance of his, Lorenzo Steward, who worked for PATH, could probably arrange for Paul to work off some of his community service hours there. Bobby Joe liked the idea and, unbeknownst to Paul, he ultimately agreed to advance Steward one hundred dollars cash. What that cash was for was less than clear, however, because Williams first introduced Steward as someone who could help repair air conditioners in Bobby Joe's various businesses, an attractive idea to Bobby Joe, since he was in need of such help at that time.

Three types of tape contamination were evident in this case: contaminating the recording, manipulating when to record and when not to, and manipulating electronic static to occur at crucial points.

Contaminating the Recording

The defense attorneys immediately suspected that, at minimum, the seven blank tapes had been tampered with. They also noticed the many on/off signatures on the remaining five tapes, especially when such signatures occurred in the midst on ongoing conversations. The last two taped conversations took place in several locations with many people constantly arriving and leaving. Williams said many things that, if Paul were present to hear them, might well implicate him in criminal activity. Since the recordings were of such low auditory quality, the problem for both the defense and the prosecution was not only how to determine who said what but also to discover who was even present at the time it was said. A videotape might have clarified such a question but this type of recording was not feasible when the cooperating witness was walking and driving around between ranches, fields, and businesses, talking with dozens of people indoors and outdoors, and frequently changing his participants. No hidden camera could be placed to capture such events effectively.

Even with only audiotape evidence, however, there are important clues about when Paul was a participant in the conversations and when he was not.

Evidence of Paul's Participating Presence

- When Paul responded and showed by his response that he had heard what was said.
- When Paul greeted or was greeted, and said good-bye or was said good-bye to.
- When there were only two people in the conversation and Paul was one of them.
- When Paul was addressed by name.
- When the pronouns "you" and "your" were used with Paul rather than "he" or "his."

Evidence of Paul's nonpresence and nonparticipation:

- When Paul did not respond to a statement or question that had no identifiable addressee.
- When Paul's voice was not heard over long stretches of conversation.
- When there were sounds of walking or moving around, which can only be from the person wearing the mike.

- When Paul was not addressed by name and was talked about as though he was not present.
- When pronoun references to Paul were "he" and "his" rather than "you" and "your."
- When Paul's voice could be heard in the distance talking with somebody else or talking on the telephone.
- When Williams's voice could be heard talking with somebody else present or on the telephone.

These clues helped determine when Paul was present and, if he was in the area, whether he was sufficiently within hearing range to participate in what was going on. In the second to last tape, Paul moved in and out of various conversations that began at Bobby Joe's ranch, then moved to a number of other sites. Williams had set this meeting up for Bobby Joe to meet with Steward about fixing his air conditioners. By chance, Paul happened to be at one of these sites also. This is the first of the only two tapes on which Paul's participation was relevant and in which his voice can be heard.

Since Steward was late for this meeting, Paul and Williams discussed a number of topics while they waited for him, all of which were small talk totally unrelated to anything illegal. Over an hour later, Steward arrived and Williams introduced him to Paul. For the first time, Paul was told how Steward might be able to help him get community service hours at PATH. Paul explained how he runs a manufacturing plant and that it's difficult for him to put in his community service hours and still manage the company he owned. Paul's voice was then not on tape for a couple minutes while Williams explained to Steward that "they had a big-head hundred" and that they need to get a hundred hours of community service. During this time, Williams referred to Paul as "he" and to the Manziel brothers as "they." Bobby Joe had been elsewhere doing something else for the previous thirty minutes and the pronoun references and lack of Paul's voice indicated that Paul had wandered off briefly to do something around the ranch. Then suddenly, Williams loudly addressed Paul by name: "Paul, how many houses do you own in this town?" Paul's voice could be heard answering, first from a distance and then growing louder as he apparently approached Williams. This gave a strong indication that he was not a participant in the preceding dialogue about the "big-head hundred." Williams clearly tried to bring

Paul back into the conversation to make it appear that he had heard what Williams just said to Steward. But the vocal signals belie that fact. Paul was not a participant at that time.

In group conversations, addressees are commonly switched. Four people can be talking together for a while, then break off into dyads. Note also how once Williams addressed Paul, he did not continue the topic of the "big-head hundred." Instead he used the hit-and-run strategy, changing the topic quickly to how many houses Paul owns.

About an hour and a half into this conversation, with Bobby Joe and Paul intermittently coming and going while Williams and Steward talked with each other, a door could be heard closing. For the next thirty minutes, until the tape is finally turned off, only Williams and Steward could be heard on tape talking with each other. Steward clearly agreed with Williams's request to help Paul obtain additional hours for his community service. The most revealing parts of this tape occur after the sound of the door closing indicated that Paul had left:

> *Williams*: See that, boy, you got your envelope.
> *Steward*: I got my envelope.
> *Williams*: When I told him I said pull that envelope out there, they didn't have that envelope for you for two weeks. Until I could catch you. Was that big-head hundred in there?
> *Steward*: I ain't never even looked at it.
> *Williams*: It's there.

Steward got the one hundred dollars but the taped evidence did not show that Paul had any knowledge that he got it or about what the money was for. Nor did this alleged critical conversation reveal that the one hundred dollars was for Steward to cook the books to show that Paul was getting community service credit that he was not entitled to have.

Manipulating When to Record

Williams's favorite technique seemed to be to put the bad stuff on tape when Paul was just out of hearing range. In one conversation, which took place largely outdoors, Williams was having trouble with his truck. When he couldn't get it started, Paul said, "Let me have that wrench," and apparently got under the hood. Once there, he could be heard shouting from a distance, "You got the key on?" indicating his location under the truck's hood. Williams then told Steward how lucky he was to now be associated with the Manziel family so that he can be paid to fix the books:

> Williams: Hey, they paid you your money to get that community service thing done, didn't they? Lorenzo, I make a lot of money with these boys.
> Steward: I know. I gotta make sure I could use some of it.

A lot depended on what "get that community service thing done" meant here. Williams tried to make it look like they were paying Steward to cook the books, but during the ten minutes that Paul was trying to get the truck started, Bobby Joe returned and made it clear to Steward that nobody would be used as Paul's substitute to do the service work, that Paul had to do it himself, and that in return for the inconvenience to Steward for his having to go to PATH to sign Paul in and out on Saturdays when Steward isn't on duty and isn't getting paid, he will get some air conditioner repair work from Bobby Joe. This was the clearest statement about what the "big-head hundred" was actually for:

> Bobby Joe: This isn't how I want to do with Paul. What I want to do is sign in and sign out. We can't send any men down there to work. What I want you to do is sign him in and sign him out. And we're not sending any help down there. Just we're not going to do it. That's my little brother. That's all we do and we can take care of you all the time. And we'll have you on one end and he's teaching school on the other end. You go sign him in and sign him out and it'll be every Saturday.

Manipulating Static at Crucial Points

It is well known among law enforcement agencies that sensitive microphones can create static noise very easily. The sound of walking creates a whoosh-whoosh noise that can interfere with any simultaneous speech. The same type of static noise can be created by moving ones arms or shuffling within position. Even the government's own transcripts record evidence of such movement. Even on the government's own transcript, "Walking sound" static is transcribed once every two pages and "Rustle" static is transcribed once every 2.4 pages. Williams was very active in causing static on the tape. "Walking" and "Rustle" together gave an average of one static instance on every page of the transcripts.

Undercover operations have encountered such difficulties frequently enough in the past to cause those who wear the hidden mikes to become very conscious of how crucial inculpatory language can be lost through such movements and actions. This awareness makes it all the more surprising that cooperating witness Williams was permitted to obscure the speech of targets throughout this operation. Sometimes such blocking may be accidental, but when it happens on a large scale, as it did in this case, and especially when it happens at times when targets appear to be starting to say something that would indicate their innocence, one can question the intentions of the person controlling the mike. The tapes in this case are replete with such created static. It is beyond the scope of this chapter to list them all. Instead, only an example will be given here.

One of the many such instances of creating static that blocked the target's response took place on May 30, the very last tape submitted in evidence, when Paul was consecutively recorded more than on any other occasion—for a total of four straight minutes. Williams asked Paul whether Steward was "taking care of" his community service. Paul responded:

> *Paul Manziel:* He's working on it . . . he's got me folding some envelopes . . . he gives me eight hours' credit to do six boxes . . .
> *Williams:* That don't take no eight hours to do it.
> *Paul Manziel:* I'm gonna knock this shit out. I've got 120 hours teaching already and Steward has got me twenty something. Yeah, but see, I have to do some work for him to get my hours.
> *Williams:* Oh, he'll slip you some in there. I'll talk to him . . . He can work it out.
> *Paul Manziel:* Uh-huh. I've already done six cartons for him. Six in forty-eight hours I've already done for him . . . so he owes me some hours.

Williams: Can't you get a occupational license over there to drive? You need to transfer yourself to Henderson County . . . say you moved over there.

Paul Manziel: But, uh (*static sounds drown out the rest of this*)

In the first part of this passage, Williams was obviously trying to get Paul to say either that he was not actually doing his community service work for PATH or that he was willing to cheat on his hours. This effort clearly failed, since Paul explained that he was working off his service hours legitimately. After Williams claimed that Steward could "slip" some hours in, Paul responded in a way in which he seemed to understand this to mean that he had already worked hours for which he hadn't been credited, apparently missing Williams's intent. So Williams took another tack, suggesting that Paul could get his unrestricted driver's license back if he would change his residence to another county. Paul started to respond with "but," a marker usually indicating that a disagreement or objection will follow. Before he could say his next word, however, loud static, followed by walking sounds, drowned out the recording and we are unable to hear the rest of Paul's statement. Williams apparently manipulated his tape recorder in order to block Paul's response.

Before Paul Manziel's trial for bribery even began, his attorneys requested that they be permitted to examine the recording equipment worn by Williams to determine whether it was fraudulently manipulated. The court agreed with this request and issued an order compelling the prosecution to provide it to the defense. After weeks of pleading with the FBI to honor the order, the prosecution reported to the court that FBI Headquarters in Quantico, Virginia, refused to comply, citing national security concerns.

Linguistic analysis can only point out the language oddities of passages of conversation when such passages are irrelevantly chopped up. Although linguistic analysis is important evidence of manipulating the recording and creating static, the ultimate test would be to let the defense examine the recording equipment to electronically determine the ways in which tape manipulation could have taken place. This refusal to make the recording device available for inspection by the defense led the judge to report that she would either suppress the tapes made by this device, the only concrete evidence in the prosecution's case, and dismiss the charges against Paul Manziel, or let the case go to trial and, in the judge's own words, "let the defense beat up on you all." Since FBI agents freely handed the device over to the cooperating witness, who had a criminal record and who was allowed to keep it in his possession for ten days without obvious supervision, the judge expressed puzzlement at the prosecutor's excuse that this was a national security case noting, "I'm unable to wrestle with this claim of national security."

I will be quick to point out that it was the cooperating witness, not law enforcement officers, who was primarily responsible for contaminating the recording process in this case. As a rule, the FBI is not guilty of such manipulation. Once in a while, however, the overwhelming desire to capture a criminal may overcome the need to be objective and aboveboard in such efforts.

10

Scripting by Requesting Directives and Apologies in a Sexual Misconduct Case: *Idaho v. J. Mussina*

In the spring of 1993, a middle-aged woman came to the clinic of Dr. Joseph Mussina, a Boise physician who specialized in abortions (all names and places have been changed here, at the request for privacy by both the defense attorney and his client). Like many other physicians, Dr. Mussina had quit doing obstetrics because of the rising cost of malpractice insurance and the increasing litigiousness of American society. The woman, Ms. Selima Kenaka, a native Nigerian, had made use of the doctor's services in January of the same year. She and her husband had visited the office together, although it is unclear whether or not the husband was aware that an abortion had been performed or that his wife had lost the baby naturally. In March, Ms. Kenaka came to the doctor's office again, this time alone. In that visit Dr. Mussina found her pregnant again. According to the doctor, Ms. Kenaka requested a second abortion.

Dr. Mussina's standard procedure was to receive payment in advance of any medical procedure. After Ms. Kenaka informed him that she had no money, he advised her to return later with the required payment, at which time he would perform the abortion. She left his office at 4:30 PM and returned an hour or so later, asking to use his telephone. At that time his office hours were over and the doctor was alone. She made a telephone call to somebody, speaking in her native language, apparently asking that person to come pick her up, then she left the clinic again. At approximately 6:30 PM, Dr. Mussina left his office and, as he approached his car in the parking lot, he saw Ms. Kenaka standing there. She explained that her ride had not come for her and that she feared that she would not be able to get a ride home. The doctor appeared to be stuck with her. He was already late for dinner but he reasoned that the only humane thing to do was to drive her home himself.

The woman and the doctor offer very different accounts of what happened on the way to her home. They agreed that she said she was hungry and wanted to stop at a fast-food drive-in on the way to her house. The doctor accommodated this wish, pulling into a drive-in and waiting in his car while the woman purchased four take-out hamburgers. After she got back into the car, the drive to her home was surprisingly short. This puzzled the doctor, since she could have easily walked that distance in two or three minutes.

Their stories differ about what happened next. The doctor reported that while he was driving, the woman began to feel his leg and offer him oral sex. He opined that she was offering to trade sex for the cost of the abortion she wanted. The doctor said that he pushed her hand away and rejected her offer. Ms. Kenaka never mentioned this event in her police reports or in her testimony. Instead, she claimed that the doctor was guilty of sexual misconduct while they were still in his office, which the doctor denied vehemently.

Two weeks after Dr. Mussina drove her home, the woman telephoned the doctor, tape-recording the conversation and telling him that she was in "great pain" and that she wanted him to prescribe some kind of medication to relieve it. She also asked him if he was angry with her. After he answered, "no," she said, "I thought maybe because I didn't put your prick in my mouth that you were angry." As the tape reveals, she spoke quickly and unclearly with a strong foreign accent, making it questionable whether the doctor comprehended or even heard her words, "prick in my mouth." She made the recording on a low-quality microcassette recorder.

After this original phone call, the woman made a multitude of calls to the doctor's office. She chose to record six of these (or perhaps preserved only six of those she recorded). The six calls were the evidence used against the doctor. Within a few weeks, his attorney sent me the six evidence tapes for my analysis.

In the six tapes the woman represented two problems. One was her medical condition (pain and bleeding). The other was the problem that she was having with her husband, who suspected her of having a boyfriend. The doctor responded with advice on both topics but gave no indication that he had done anything wrong with her. If he had said something like, "I loved it when you did that to me," the prosecution would have had something tangible to work with. But he didn't even come close to this.

Curiously, Ms. Kenaka began her tapes with denials that oral sex had ever occurred and later tapes with denials that she would ever tell her husband about it. In a case in which the whole point of the taping was to capture guilt on tape, it seemed odd that the woman would begin by denying that oral sex had ever happened. But suppose the doctor had replied with something like, "I really enjoyed it," or "Let's do it again sometime," or "That's our little secret." What speakers *could* have said but didn't is often as salient as what they actually said. The doctor was mystified by what she was saying and offered no confirmation that he understood her or agreed with what she said.

When the doctor failed to incriminate himself this way, the woman began to try a scripting strategy, primarily to get him to give her directives about what she should tell her husband. This conversational strategy was used throughout the first five tapes:

Call number	Ms. Kenaka	Dr. Mussina's Response
1	What do I say? What do I tell him?	Well, you might have miscarried, you know.
	What do you want me to tell him?	
		Well, just tell him that you started bleeding, you know, that's all.
3	He said I was talking to you yesterday.	
		You just tell him that you had a pain and that's why you were calling.

3	If he gets back to me, what do I do?	
		Okay, let me, I will call you back, okay?
4	What do you expect me to tell him?	
		You tell me.
4	He wants me to get out of the house. Where do I go?	
		Listen, if you have problems, then you tell me. I will go out and make an arrangement for you to stay, okay?
4	I mean just tell me what you want me to do [*sobbing*]	
		If you keep on crying I cannot listen to you.
5	When my husband leaves me, you will not be ready for me, is that right?	
		Why should I be?

The prosecution tried to make the doctor's response, "I'll call you back," appear to indicate that he was so involved that he couldn't think of a good answer at the time. Throughout that tape, however, Dr. Mussina had indicated that he was in the middle of an important consultation and that he didn't have time to talk with her then. Likewise, the prosecution believed that the "arrangement" that the doctor said he'd make was an intimate one. But this was a doctor who also owned a number of motels in that city and he was merely telling her that he'd find her a room so that she wouldn't have to sleep on the street. Dr. Mussina apparently began to tumble about what the woman was really up to when she asked if he would "be ready for" her. To this he gave a functional "no" response, "Why should I be?"

Ms. Kenaka had tape-recorded the first five tapes completely on her own. At this point she went to the police and showed them the tapes. They apparently decided that there wasn't enough on them to indict Dr. Mussina, so they instructed her to record one more conversation, this time using a different version of the scripting conversational strategy, that of requesting the doctor's apology. It is altogether logical to believe that people who apologize for an offense have actually committed it. But, as the doctor's responses to these requests show, the act of apologizing is very complex. What may seem on the surface to be an apology is often not one at all. Apologies commonly are made by someone who has committed an offense against another. But there are also other apparent apologies that simply express regret that an offensive act has occurred, such as "I'm sorry that it rained yesterday and ruined your picnic" or "I'm sorry that you have a bad cold." In such cases, the alleged apologizer is in no way responsible for the offense. These can hardly qualify as actual apologies. Another important factor in an apology is that both speakers must have the same reference about what the apology is all about. The following are the efforts of Ms. Kenaka to get Dr. Mussina to apologize:

Ms. Kenaka	Dr. Mussina's Response
I thought you were going to say you were sorry for what happened.	
	What?
You should have told him maybe he should bring me.	
	Okay, I'm sorry for that.
You are sorry for what you did to me?	
	Yes, I am sorry.
I want you to apologize to me.	
	For what?
For what you did to me that night. For putting your prick in my mouth while I was sleeping.	
	Okay, I'm busy now.
Tell me, "I'm sorry" and just tell me something now that just makes me feel I should forgive you and don't talk about it again.	
	Okay, I'm sorry.
Sorry for putting your prick in my mouth.	
	I'm sorry if you feel like that.
Are you sorry for that? Just say	

yes or no. Are you sorry for that or are you sorry just for sorry's sake?	
	I told you already.
That you are sorry for what happened that night? You say you are sorry and I don't know why you are sorry.	
	I'll talk to you later.
Just say you are sorry for that . . . for what happened.	
	Come see me. We'll talk.
I ask you if you are sorry for what you did to me. I don't know why you are sorry. I have to be satisfied too.	
	I already told you.
Sorry for what happened.	
	Okay, bye.

Clearly the most promising evidence against the doctor was achieved through this conversational strategy. During the week of the trial, the prosecutor appeared on local television claiming that the doctor evidenced his guilt through his many apologies. Although Dr. Mussina warded off most of these requests for an apology, the woman did get him to apologize felicitously three times:

1. for the fact that he did not insist that her husband accompany her on her visit to his clinic;
2. for the fact that she feels "like that";
3. for what he "did to" her "that night."

Referencing can help with the first apology. Her husband did accompany her in her January visit to the doctor's office. He clearly did not accompany her in her March visit, when she had nobody to drive her home. When she asked the doctor to apologize for not insisting that her husband accompany her, therefore, the doctor was in total agreement. If he only had done so, it would have avoided his having to drive her home. Apologizing for this was a piece of cake. But this apology had no salience for the prosecution's case. For one thing, the doctor apologized for something that he did not do, not for something he did. Second, the apology was benign in terms of the charges against him. The prosecutor could, indeed, claim that the doctor apologized, but once he might try to explain what the apology was all about, his point would seem laughable.

The second alleged apology was not a genuine apology at all. To say that he is sorry that she feels that way is to admit no more than saying, "I'm sorry" to a person whose pet has just died. It is an expression of sympathy, not an apology.

In the doctor's third apology, if there were a mutual understanding of "what you did to me that night," the case for the doctor might have been bleak. But the woman had consistently muddied the possibility of a mutual understanding with her own referencing. The possibilities of "that night" were:

1. The late-afternoon abortion procedure in January, which she requested and paid for almost three months before her March visit to his office.
2. The late afternoon in March when she claimed that he either attempted oral sex or completed it in his office, depending on to whom she had testified earlier. Her initial claim to the police was that the act was consummated but, in a later police interview, she said that the doctor had only attempted it. Still later, she reversed herself and claimed that the act had actually taken place. With such conflicting claims, the prosecutor decided to charge the doctor only with the attempt, not with the completed act.
3. The March incident, later in the evening, after her visit to the doctor's office, when she didn't bring payment for the procedure and after which the doctor drove her home, thus making the husband suspect that the doctor was her boyfriend.

Obviously, the woman wanted the doctor to understand that "that night" referred to the March afternoon incident (number two above) and, more specifically, to this alleged attempt to force oral sex on her. The doctor's understanding of "that night" could have been any of these three time references. His testimony was that he was uncertain whether she was referring to her January abortion (number one above), which he believed she had represented to her husband not as an abortion but as a miscarriage, or to his driving her home (number three above), which allegedly caused her to have marital problems because she was seen with the doctor in his car. However unjustified the woman may have been in blaming the doctor for either incident, Dr. Mussina maintained that he was willing to tell her anything just to keep her from tying up his telephone line while he was busy with his patients in the office.

Although the conversational strategy of scripting generally begins with directives about what the other person should say, Ms. Kenaka modified it here with her requests for directives and requests for an apology. In a sense, she was scripting his response by demanding the speech acts that he should use to answer her. Using the analysis presented here, Dr. Mussina was acquitted of all charges.

PART III

Uses by Law Enforcement Officers

This section describes criminal law cases in which undercover law enforcement officers use conversational power strategies on their targets. They use most of the same strategies as the ones employed by cooperating witnesses but, unlike them, the police lean a bit more heavily on the strategies of camouflaging their representations of illegality by making them appear to be legal and making use of the hit-and-run strategy.

11

Police Camouflaging in an Obstruction of Justice Case: *US v. Brian Lett*

In February 2001 a young Canadian lawyer named Brian Lett, just recently out of law school, inadvertently walked into trouble when his new client, Thomas Crain, got entangled in a Minnesota telemarketing fraud case. Lett was charged with obstruction of justice and conspiring to commit obstruction of justice. The prosecution alleged that Lett and his client, Crain, suggested to an undercover officer posing as a Visa fraud investigator and using the name Terrence Edwards, that they wanted Edwards to steal investigative records from the U.S. Postal Service and use some unexplained influence to remove the US Postal Inspector from the case. Part of Edwards's role in the case was to help Lett get copies of documents showing how his client was being charged. Edwards tape-recorded two conversations in which it was alleged that Lett was trying to do two things:

1. Steal the investigative records from the U.S. Postal Service, and
2. Use some unexplained influence to remove the U.S. Postal Inspector from the case.

The entire evidence against attorney Lett consisted of two telephone conversations on tape. One was between undercover officer Edwards and the U.S. Postal Inspector, Wanda Krueger. It did not include Lett at all. The other conversation involved Edwards talking first with attorney Lett, then with his client, Crain.

When attorneys are indicted, it is common for them to hire experienced, top-notch criminal lawyers to defend them. Lett was just out of law school, however, and had only just begun his practice. Still in debt with education expenses, he called on Scott Tilsen of the Minneapolis office of the Federal Public Defender. It was fortuitous for Lett that the experienced and competent Tilsen recognized immediately that this was a case that would depend on a linguistic analysis of the conversational strategies used in the tapes. He was concerned from the outset about who actually originated the idea to steal the records and destroy them, so he sent the tapes to me.

The early parts of the tape on which Lett and Crain can be heard show that their major interest was in learning more about the government's case against Crain by legally obtaining the appropriate files. So far, they had been stymied in getting them from a Ms. Matt in the Office of Postal Inspector and from the office of the prosecutor. Edwards posed a series of questions to Lett, alternating between ways of getting the files and ways of getting Ms. Matt and the prosecutor off the case. He began with ways of getting copies of the files:

> *Edwards*: There was a little problem with 'em because remember what you asked me about, were there any copies made of the files?
> Lett: Uh-huh.
> *Edwards*: Then what it was, I think, to the best of my understanding, is somebody was on their own trying to make copies of the files but to make a long story short, uh, Ms. Matt don't work there anymore.
> *Lett*: Do you mean she doesn't work as a postal inspector?

There was no expression of illegality here. Edwards simply said that somebody was trying to make copies on their own. Since Ms. Matt doesn't work there anymore, Lett could take this to mean that somebody else at the office of the Postal Inspector was trying to do this for Lett. Any illegality was camouflaged to make it appear to be a normal business process. Edwards was no clearer in his next representation:

> *Edwards*: Do you have a case number with the prosecutor?

> *Lett*: Uh, no, 'cause it hasn't been filed and what's happening is—
> *Edwards*: [*interrupting*] Do y'all want those retrieved too? I need to know everybody that's got files that y'all want retrieved.

We can't know what Lett was trying to say in his reply to Edwards's "what's happening," since Edwards blocked his answer by interrupting him before he could finish, asking if he wants the documents "retrieved." The most common meanings of "retrieved" are "to discover and bring in," "to get back again or regain," "to return successfully," and "to recover from storage." No dictionary definition of "retrieved" suggests that it means stolen or otherwise illegally obtained. The camouflage continued as Edwards got a bit bolder in his following representation:

> *Edwards*: Who's got files on any of this? I need to know anybody and everybody and which uses of 'em y'all want delivered to you, because those things, they gotta disappear. If you don't get rid of all of 'em, then you're gonna be stuck.
> *Lett*: Uh, well I mean the huge one right now is the prosecutor.

The topic here continued to be about various places where the files were housed. Edwards, of course, was trying to indicate that the files would have to "disappear" (presumably hinting that they had to be stolen) from where they were currently housed. But to this point there had been no clear indication, certainly not an explicit one, that the files would have to be stolen, so Lett could understand Edwards's "they gotta disappear" to mean that he had to "get rid of" the charges, which was the point of his entire effort to defend his client, Crain. If he were to get the charges against his client dropped, Lett first had to see the files. One danger with the camouflage strategy, as clearly evidenced here, is that this form of deliberate ambiguity often leads to multiple understandings.

Lett was surprised when Edwards informed him that Ms. Matt, who had previously denied him access to the files, was no longer on the case. Ostensibly to prove that this was true, Edwards then suggested that Lett call that office and ask for Ms. Matt personally. The primary reason for

Edwards to suggest this was to show Lett that he had some unidentified strong influence in that office and to hint that Ms. Matt was removed as a result of such influence.

> *Edwards*: Make you a phone call to wherever Matt's office is at, and go ahead and get your confirmation. If you want, I'll stay on the line and listen. Just tell 'em you want to make some copies, or however you want to do it, whatever you did last time. See if you can speak to her first [*laughs*]. That'd be funny.

Note that Edwards suggested that Lett tell them that he wanted "to make some copies." Wanting to make copies is not even close to stealing them. Lett agreed to make the call. He got an answering machine saying that any caller who wanted to speak with Ms. Matt should instead call Wanda Krueger, the U.S. Postal Inspector. After this, Edwards continued:

> *Edwards*: She must be gone, huh? I wonder how that happened? [*laughs*]
> *Lett*: Wow.

After Lett was indicted, the prosecution used this exchange to show that Lett knew that it was Edwards's influence that got Ms. Matt removed, an awareness that allegedly implicated Lett in a conspiracy to obstruct justice. Of course, Edwards's words did not say explicitly that he used his influence. Lett's "wow" response was interpreted by the prosecution to mean that now he was really impressed with Edwards's power and influence to make illegal things happen in the office of the U.S. Postal Inspector. But wait. There was also a perfectly benign interpretation of Lett's "wow." To him it could have meant something like, "Wow, that office sure changes personnel quickly," or "Wow, that's surprising news."

It is equally unclear how a Visa fraud inspector could have any influence at all on the U.S. Postal Inspector's office. If anything, Lett would need to have inferred that Edwards was somehow the cause of Ms. Matt's removal. When crucial evidence is left to inference, there is always the possibility of multiple understandings. Was Lett simply surprised that Ms. Matt was no longer on the case? Or did he understand that this was because of Edwards's alleged influence? No matter what the prosecution inferred, his response, "Wow," did not really answer either question.

So far in this conversation, Edwards had been fishing for Lett to say something that would implicate himself. The camouflaged use of "make copies" and "retrieve," "disappear," and "get rid of" had not yielded any evidence of Lett's conspiracy or knowledge in a conspiracy. So Edwards tried another approach, asking if Lett would like it if the prosecutor, like Ms. Matt, were removed from the case:

> *Edwards*: What do you think the best thing to do with him?
> *Lett*: Just get him to stop what he's doing.
> *Edwards*: What do you want me to do? I mean, do you want me to just have somebody call him and tell him just stop, or what?
> *Lett*: I don't know if that would make him stop though.

One of the common strategies in such undercover work is to request directives from the target. Building on the hint that he was somehow responsible for Ms. Matt's removal from the case, Edwards now asked if Lett would like to have the prosecutor removed. Lett's answer indicated that he would like to have the prosecutor "stop what he's doing," which could only mean that Lett would prefer that the prosecutor stop refusing to give Lett the files that he needs so that he can do a better job of defending his client, but he didn't think that simply telling the prosecutor to stop this would do any good.

At trial the prosecution claimed that Lett's observation about the futility of simply asking the prosecutor to stop meant that he wanted Edwards to use his influence to do something that was a great deal stronger than asking the prosecutor to stop. The prosecution's inference was that Lett wanted Edwards to use his influence to get the prosecutor to step down. But this, like much of the case to this point, was an inference, and inferences are a long way from the explicitness required in a successful prosecution.

Apparently realizing that he was getting nowhere with his effort to get Lett to agree for him to use his unidentified, alleged influence, Edwards shifted to stating both goals at the same time—stealing the files and having the prosecutor removed:

Edwards: Just see if I can get a hold of the files? Or do you want him transferred?
Lett: Just so that he's, I just, really I don't know, I don't care how it's done. Just, just, if he, if something can be done to just to get the guy off, off his back, you know, off Crain's back, that would be good.
Edwards: Well, the only thing about doing the same thing to him that was done to Ms. Matt is, uh, it would take somebody puttin' pressure on him and then somebody actually obtaining the files that he's got.
Lett: I think that, yeah, that, that sounds good. If it can be done.

Here was another opportunity for Edwards to be explicit about his intentions. Instead of saying, "get a hold of the files," and "obtaining the files," he could have said, "Just see if I can steal the files." But he doesn't. He's still hoping that Lett will catch his euphemistic expression and eventually incriminate himself. Nor did Edwards's "puttin' pressure on him" give any clear indication of whether this meant using illegal influence or simply repairing the prosecutor's sense of the injustice he caused by not sharing the information needed by Lett for adequately defending his client. So when Lett said, "that sounds good," Edwards had still not caught his fish. So he upped the ante even more with the following:

Edwards: Okay, well let me tell you something now. Uh, we're talking about, we, we're talking about, I got somebody stealing these files.
(short pause)
Lett: Oh.
Edwards: They have to be destroyed. You understand that, don't you? Because they don't exist no more.
Lett: But who, who, where are they going then? I'm talking about Ms. Matt.
Edwards: I thought you wanted them at your office.
Lett: Yeah, I do, but I mean, okay I just wanted to know and then—

Edwards: (*interrupting*) Didn't Craiǻn say he needed to go through them or something?
Lett: No. We can, I mean, I don't know. I don't think it's, you know, as long as it's done, done with, then that's fine.

Finally Edwards appeared to recognize that he hadn't been getting through to Lett with words like "get," "retrieve," and "obtain." His "Okay, well let me tell you something" is evidence that the "something" he was about to tell Lett would clarify any past misunderstanding. He didn't say "You knew this before," or "I've told you this before." His "okay" is a discourse marker indicating that a new, clarifying topic was forthcoming here.

So Edwards now introduced for the first time the explicit verb, "steal." Lett's response, "Oh," confirms that this is new information to him. As a discourse marker, "oh" indicates that the speaker undergoes some kind of change in his current state of knowledge, information, orientation, or awareness (Schiffrin 1987; Heritage 1984). Fraser (1999) points out that "oh" in such a context has at least three distinct roles: as an interjection ("Oh! I wasn't aware of that), a kind of pause filler ("There were, oh, about 20 or so"), and as an emotional pause marker ("Oh Harry, why don't you just shut up"). It is clear that Lett's use of "Oh" here corresponds to Fraser's first role as an interjection of surprise.

But also Edwards added, "they have to be destroyed," then did a quick hit and run saying, "You understand that, don't you? Because they don't exist no more." Lett, still reeling from the new information, agreed that he understood this tag question (which law tends to call a leading question). Every attorney who cross-examines a witness will agree that tag questions of this type are difficult to disagree with. In fact, that's precisely why they are used.

After he absorbed this, Lett's off-topic response was to ask where Ms. Matt's files were going. Lett's "I just wanted to know and then—" is interrupted by Edwards. What is it that Lett just wanted to know? Even though we can't learn this when it is blocked by interruption, even the start of this interrupted question is consistent with what had been said to this point—that Lett was trying to say that he just wanted to know what happened to the files that were in Ms. Matt's office. He did not know that the only copy of the files had allegedly been taken.

Lett's responses were discombobulated. Lett was not an accomplished speaker, and had trouble processing new information quickly. He was brand new to the practice of law. He was no match for Edwards's strategies of camouflage and confusion. He didn't know whether or not his client wanted to "go through" the files. He concluded, "as long as it's done with, then that's fine," more an effort to get disentangled from a troublesome conversation than an admission of guilt. The jury agreed, acquitting him of all charges.

12

Police Camouflaging in a Purchasing Stolen Property Case: US v. Tariq Shalash

The Shalash family, recently emigrated from the Middle East, opened and operated a wholesale grocery business in Lexington, Kentucky. As Mohammed Shalash, the father, grew older, he turned over most of the operation to his sons, Tariq and Ziyad Shalash. This particular type of wholesale grocery was one that engaged in purchasing large quantities of diverse goods and merchandise from various parties, then repackaging and selling them for a profit at retail. Among other things, the Shalash family dealt in foodstuffs, detergents, baby food, health products, beauty aids, razors, and other small items. One method they used to find such products was to locate overstocks from other businesses and to negotiate a price for taking the merchandise off of their hands. Another method was to purchase merchandise from the manufacturers directly or from middlemen entrepreneurs who had previously purchased such overstock from the manufacturers.

The commercial practice of repurchasing and repackaging merchandise caught the attention of Kentucky law enforcement officers, who believed that this type of business held high potential for owners to purchase stolen property such as high-jacked trailer loads of goods. Indeed, in 2000, Pfizer Inc., the manufacturer of Viagra, suspected that such activity was taking place in Lexington, Kentucky. Acting in an undercover capacity, Pfizer's director of corporate security, Aaron Graham, contacted Tariq Shalash, asking to trade his load of Enfamil infant formula for any Viagra that Tariq might have on hand or to which he might have access. Tariq explained that he couldn't sell Viagra, since he was not licensed to do so, but that he would trade the small amount that he had on hand for some of Graham's Enfamil. Graham then asked for the assistance of the Memphis Auto/Cargo Theft Task Force to help him obtain the large quantities of Enfamil that he promised to use in the trade. Three transactions were then made in March and April 2001, only the first of which involved Viagra in a trade.

After an indictment was brought, Shalash's defense attorney, Robert Webb of Louisville, called on me to help with the analysis of the tape recordings of conversations between Tariq and the undercover agents. In the initial transaction on March 15, 2001, a Memphis police department officer, acting in an undercover capacity and using the alias, Paul Sherman, drove a semi-trailer containing three pallets of Enfamil baby formula to Tariq Shalash's workplace with the intent to consummate the proposed trade of Enfamil for Viagra. Tariq gave Sherman the fifty-three bottles of Viagra (thirty pills in each bottle) that he had on hand as partial payment in this uneven exchange. To make up the difference in value, Tariq wrote Sherman a check for six thousand dollars, representing the value of the Enfamil, worth sixteen thousand dollars, deducting some ten thousand dollars, the value of the Viagra. Sherman then asked Tariq to cash this check for him, which he did. Before he left, Sherman told Tariq that he could get more shipments like this and come back again.

A month later, Sherman returned with a semi-trailer load of cereal and hair-care products. Sherman asked Tariq for Viagra in exchange, but Tariq said he didn't have it and couldn't get any. Sherman claimed that he told Tariq that the cereal was stolen, although the tapes of the meeting did not make this at all clear. Tariq wrote Sherman a personal check for thirty thousand dollars, then cashed it for him in the same way that he did in the first transaction. As he left, Sherman again advised Tariq, using these exact words, that he could "pick off" more loads of merchandise that he would like to trade for Viagra.

Two weeks later, the third transaction took place. Sherman telephoned Tariq while allegedly en route from Ohio, telling him that he had "grabbed" another load of merchandise for Tariq to consider buying.

Again Sherman pleaded for Viagra in exchange, and again Tariq said he didn't have any. Following the same procedure, after paying some thirty-seven thousand dollars for the new load, Sherman asked Tariq to cash his check, which he again did. Before he left, Sherman asked Tariq what else he might want next time. Tariq told him that his number one product was baby formula milk, but that he was also interested in Motrin and Tylenol. This statement was used in the indictment, but reformulated to say that Tariq had aided and abetted the crime by requesting a laundry list of items he would be willing to purchase.

It is clear that Tariq did indeed trade Viagra to Sherman without benefit of a license. In the indictment, Tariq was also accused of originating the whole transaction, as follows:

> ... defendants herein did counsel, induce, and cause other persons to transport, transmit, and transfer ... goods then known to him to be stolen ... one hundred cases of Enfamil.

The tape-recorded evidence did not support Tariq as the inducer and causer, however, as the following conversation shows:

> *Graham*: I have samples of Enfamil and Similac *I'd love to bring down* to you ... We have some huge quantities so I want *to bring 'em down* and show 'em to you. You tell me what they're worth and then maybe do some business.
> *Tariq*: Yeah, sure.
> *Graham*: Tell me, if I come in Thursday afternoon should I call you at the office when I get into the area?
> *Tariq*: Yeah, call me.
> *Graham*: *I'll bring my stuff* and show you what we have. I have a couple of trucks of this stuff.

This conversation shows that it was Graham who "counseled, induced, and caused" here, rather than Tariq, who passively agreed to the suggestions or inducements made by the agent. Note also that there was nothing in what Graham said to indicate that the merchandise had been stolen. Apparently, Graham left this task for Sherman to accomplish in his follow-up deliveries to Tariq.

Camouflaging the Source of the Merchandise

Since the initial conversations with Graham did not represent that the merchandise was stolen, the issue became whether or not the undercover policeman who was to deliver the goods, Paul Sherman, was unambiguous and clear about it or whether he camouflaged his source as well as his method of obtaining the merchandise. It is clear from the indictment that the government's case would hinge largely on the alleged representation by the agents that the goods were indeed stolen. Evidence of this position can be seen in the indictment's 63 uses of the expressions, "stolen," "stolen goods," "steal," and "stole." Throughout the series of undercover tapes in this case, however, the two undercover police officers were not explicit about the source of the alleged stolen merchandise. They referred to it as "the truck," "the people," "somebody," "some friends," "these people," "we," "they," "a boy," and an unidentified man named Juan, as the following passages illustrate:

> *Graham:* Here's what we'll do. I'll just have *the truck* bring the milk to you and then I'll call you and tell you when the product will be there.
>
> * * *
>
> *Graham:* So I talked to *the people* that, that's got the stuff for us.
>
> * * *
>
> *Graham:* I had *somebody* call me and say they had these products. He just told me about the products.
>
> * * *
>
> *Graham:* I have *some friends* that have it, and that's where I got the stuff that came today.
>
> * * *
>
> *Graham:* *These people* told me this Visine, Listerine, Halls, and Lubriderm were available.
>
> * * *
>
> *Sherman:* *Juan* told me to show it to you. If you want it, he'll sell it to you. He always gets that stuff.
>
> * * *
>
> *Sherman:* It's hard to find. You have to know when it's coming in. If you want it, I try to find it. *We* got a Kellogg's plant down there.

They pull them trailers up there. It's easy. I can get you all of that. But if I can find a trailer load of it, I'll take it and bring it to you if you'll take it.

* * *

Sherman: I know *a boy* right now that's got some, uh, Motrin.

* * *

Sherman: *We* got these warehouses down there man. Get all the cereal, I can bring you all the cereal you want.

* * *

Sherman: That *boy*, he called me the other day. He told me that he had, uh, he knew where a whole thing of Motrin was.

* * *

Sherman: If *he* tells me something, *he's* right. [unintelligible] big parking lot over there. You can get anything you want.

* * *

Sherman: *He* don't lie to me. If *he* says he knows where it's at, *he* knows where it's at.

* * *

Sherman: A thousand ways to get it. I mean, you got your *contacts*, I got mine. And *he* calls me and I'm gonna call you. If I can get it, I'll bring it.

Where the agents got the merchandise was also never made explicit and clear. Perhaps Tariq should have insisted on knowing this, but if his purchase of merchandise from sellers like these was standardly legitimate, there would have been no reason to think that on this occasion he should be aware of anything different. People who expect things to be normal often don't bother to anticipate an aberrant situation. It is likely that the agents in this case counted on this.

Camouflaging How the Merchandise Was Obtained

Nor were the police officers clear and unambiguous about how the alleged stolen goods were obtained. In the vast majority of cases they used ambiguous verbs such as "get/got," "have/had," "come/came/coming," "look (around) for," "were available," "pick up," and "find/found," as the following passages illustrate:

Graham: So I talked to the people that's *got* the stuff for us.

* * *

Graham: I had somebody call me and say they *had* these products.

* * *

Graham: I'll *look around for* some more of that but I have some friends that have it and that's where I *got* the stuff that *came* today, so I'll *look around* for some more.

* * *

Graham: These people told me this Visine, Listerine, Halls, and Lubriderm *were available*.

* * *

Graham: I'll *look for* some more sources for that.

* * *

Sherman: I think he's *got* some more *comin'*. He always *gets* that stuff. I've *got* something else up there.

* * *

Sherman: He told me to call him if you need us to *pick anything up* or something.

* * *

Sherman: I know they *got* it though.

* * *

Sherman: I *got* seventy-five cases.

* * *

Sherman: If you want it, we *got* it.

* * *

Sherman: I *got* sixty cases of these. I *got* those little A&D ointment travel packs. I *got*, uh, twenty-four boxes, I *got* seventy-five cases of those.

* * *

Sherman: You have to know where it's *comin'* and when it's *comin'* and they you just stand at the door.

* * *

Sherman: I tell you what I *got* and you tell me if you want it.

* * *

Sherman: It's hard to find. I try to *find* it. I can *get* all you want of that. You got to find out when it's *comin'*. But if I can *find* a trailer load of it, I'll take it and bring it to you, if you'll take it.

* * *

Sherman: I know a boy right now that's *got* some.

* * *

Sherman: We *got* these warehouses down there man. *Get* all the cereal I can bring you. Anything I *bring* you will be legit.

* * *

Sherman: I try to *get* all that I can. I'm gonna *get* that Motrin to you. Anytime. I'll bring it.

* * *

Sherman: He's right in that big parkin' lot over there. You can *get* anything you want.

* * *

Sherman: Thousand ways to *get* it. I'm gonna call you if I can *get* it.

* * *

Sherman: I *got* some stuff I want to bring to you. I *got* some other stuff too. I *got* some Listerine. I've *got* some Lubriderm. I *got* some Hall's Cough Drops too.

* * *

Sherman: I *got* that Motrin man. You want me to tell you what I *got*? I've *got* these eleven pallets. I *got* some more, uh, uh, uh, formula too.

There can be some legitimate disagreement about Sherman's meaning of "get" and "got." In two of the above statements he says "I've got," which can be equivalent to "I have," irrespective of how he got it. But when he says "I got" and "I'll get" every other time, it is at least plausible that Sherman believed that he used this verb to indicate that he "got" it or "will get it" in a less than honest way. Regardless of what Sherman intended "got" to mean, the verb denotes many other perfectly legal things, including "possessed," "owned," "obtained," "found," "located," "discovered," "sought out," "prepared," "received," "seized," or "found," none of which specify illegality. People determine meaning from context. In this context, it is unlikely that Sherman intended to mean that he bought or owned the warehouse or truckload. The meaning most likely here is that he found, located, or discovered one. If Sherman had wanted to be explicit here, he could have said that this warehouse or truckload is a good place to steal goods. But he apparently preferred to camouflage illegality with benign and ambiguous expressions.

At the very end of the undercover investigation, probably because the police realized that they had not been clear and unambiguous about the origins of their merchandise, Sherman grew a bit bolder and used three verbs that the prosecution must have thought did a better job of representing that the merchandise had actually been stolen: "pick off," "grabbed," and "can steal."

> Sherman: I tell you somethin' though, between me and you, that's hard to *pick off*.
>
> * * *
>
> Sherman: I *grabbed* it over in uh, West Memphis.
>
> * * *
>
> Sherman: We got a Kroger place up there and you *can steal* this shit all day long, get it and gone.

Before discussing these three statements, a simple tally of the verbs chosen by the police to suggest that the goods were stolen is as follows:

get	35
bring	12
find	4
look for	3
have	3
were available	1
pick off	1
grab	1
can steal	1

On the surface, it seems odd that only the last three of the sixty-one efforts to represent stolen merchandise in this case (4.9 percent) even approached some level of explicitness. It seems equally odd that these three verbs were not used until the end of the investigation, although this is probably because the government's review of the earlier efforts to represent illegality showed them that their efforts had fallen short. But even these three statements camouflaged the idea that the goods were stolen:

1. "That's Hard to *Pick Off*"

"Pick off" is an expression commonly used in baseball for a quick throw from a pitcher or catcher to an infielder with the purpose of catching a runner off base. In American football, a "pick off" refers to a defensive player's interception of an offensive player's forward pass. In hunting, it is used more broadly to designate the location of a target, such as "picking off a duck." The essential meaning of "pick off" is to locate something, then execute. Location of the merchandise is a necessary first step in any transaction of this type, and location of it does not communicate execution, in this case theft, which was the core of the government's case.

In the context of this case, there is little reason for the target to have suspected that "pick off" was intended to mean anything other than locating where an available shipment of merchandise might have been located before it was obtained. Further, there is little reason for the target to have understood that "obtaining" meant stealing. Tariq would first need to have developed personally a schema of illegality in order to have understood Sherman's meaning of "to steal." In the months of discussion leading up to Sherman's use of this expression, the only verbs used were "get," "look for," "find," "have," and "be available." Muddling matters even further is Tariq's possible understanding of "pick off" here, which could well have been consistent with the other fifty-nine verbs used by Sherman.

2. "I *Grabbed* It over in, uh, West Memphis."

The basic meanings of "grab," as any dictionary will attest, are: to take or grasp suddenly, to capture or restrain, as in an arrest, to obtain unscrupulously or forcibly, to take hurriedly, and to capture the attention of. Although the third sense, "to obtain unscrupulously or forcibly," is consistent with the intent of stealing, no dictionary I could locate lists "grab" as a synonym for "steal." If Sherman's intent was to indicate that he "stole" the goods here, he easily could have been clear by using the verb, "steal," or one of its common synonyms. Instead, he chose a verb that, in this context, is more appropriate to meanings one and four above, a hurried act. Hurrying is consistent with this type of commerce, since the sooner one locates and obtains the merchandise, the sooner the product then becomes no longer available to competitors to obtain and to realize a profit from its resale.

3. "We Got a Kroger Place up There You *Can Steal* This Shit All Day Long, Get It and Gone."

It is likely that upon review of the many previous tapes, the supervising agents or the prosecutor had noticed Sherman's many vague representations about the origins of the merchandise and now urged him to actually say the word, "steal," so that the source of the merchandise finally would be clear and unambiguous to Tariq. The supervisors probably also noticed that Tariq had resisted Sherman's many efforts to get them some more Viagra, which was the original intent of the whole operation. If it was made clear to Tariq that the goods were actually stolen property, the case against him would be solidified. So Sherman finally used the word here.

But several things must be said about this passage. First, the written transcript of this sentence does not tell the whole story. On the tape, Sherman lowered his voice considerably when he uttered this statement. When faced with this criticism, the prosecution can logically argue that the agent normally lowers his voice in such contexts so that any other people in the area would not be able to hear what was said. Voice lowering also adds a sense of covertness to the tape. These are possibly good reasons but, in this case, there was nobody anywhere near the two men, making it a questionable justification.

Second, and perhaps even more important, in this sentence Sherman did not actually say that the goods *had been* stolen. Instead, he used the conditional verb, "can," here. Sherman says that he "got" (not "stole") the cereal at "a Kroger place where you *can* steal this shit all day long." Sherman's "you" is equivalent to the general pronoun, "one," which, when coupled with the conditional "can," says something like, "this place is where somebody could steal the stuff any time they wanted to." The verb phrase represents an indefinite future, not a definite past.

Third, since this is the closest Sherman had come to representing that his goods were stolen, this ineloquent representation must have caught Tariq's attention, for he responded immediately as follows:

Tariq: I told him not to bring. "I don't want to use that." I told him before, "I don't want to use that."

Here Tariq reports a functional "no" response, which had been ignored in the past and now continued to be ignored by Sherman. The "him" Tariq referred to is Graham, the man who approached him in the first place and who sent Sherman to deliver the merchandise. Tariq's "I don't want" indicates that from the beginning of these transactions he had told Graham that he did not want any such merchandise in the future. "I don't want" is not conventionally used to describe past events. For example, one can't say "I don't want to go the movies last week." Here, Tariq reprised his past conversation with Graham as an indication that in the past he told Graham that he would have nothing to do with illegal goods in the present or future.

This would be a good place to comment on transcript representations of spoken language. Often the government transcripts omit quotation marks around quoted or reconstructed oral language. Putting quotes around what Tariq said here, as the defense transcript did, makes it clearer that Tariq was saying that he told this to Graham at an earlier date. There were no such quotation marks on the prosecution's transcript.

Realizing that undercover operations are based on deception, including the pretense of who the agents represent and other facts in the scenario, there is still a bright line separating camouflaged representations of illegality from essential truths that are central to criminal charges. If such representations are not offered in terms that can be clearly understood as illegal, the prosecution's case remains seriously clouded. Since I was not called to testify in this case, I don't really know whether any part of my analysis was used at trial. I was told, however, that Shalash was convicted for purchasing stolen property.

13

A Rogue Cop and Every Strategy He Can Think Of: *The Wenatchee Washington Sex Ring Case*

In 1994 a child sexual abuse investigation was launched in the rural western Washington apple-growing city of Wenatchee. By the time it was over, forty-three adults were charged with twenty-nine thousand counts of rape and molestation of sixty children. A multitude of police reports written by Wenatchee detective Robert Perez described dozens of adults lining up to take turns molesting children. Mothers, fathers, and brothers were reported to have raped their own family's children and neighbor children. Pastors and pastor's wives were said to have raped the children in their own congregations. Twenty-eight of the forty-three adults charged in these cases were convicted at trial. Doris Green was one of them. This group included not only many local poor and mentally challenged parents but also some relatively middle-class adults. Many of them signed confessions of their guilt. This appeared to be either the worst case of child sexual abuse in American history or a classic example of a terrible witch-hunt gone awry.

This saga began when social workers took a nine-year-old girl away from her parents and assigned her to live with Detective Perez and his family, who often took in foster children. According to Perez, one night this girl told him tearfully that her parents had molested her many times. Perez then elicited another accusation from the girl's older sister, who confirmed it and went on to describe how neighbors joined with her parents for sex parties, taking turns trading the children between them.

She also added that the pastor of their church used to ravish young girls on the pulpit and had them line up for sex with him. When Perez drove the nine-year-old around Wenatchee, she pointed out eighteen homes where she allegedly had been molested. The more questions Perez asked, the more terrible stories he discovered. When interviewed by Perez, many other local children told him of sex orgies and abuse by their parents and neighbors.

Interestingly, Detective Perez never tape-recorded any of these conversations and accusations. Later it was learned that he also had destroyed whatever interview notes he made. The absence of such tapes and notes became important when some of the children eventually admitted that after they recanted their stories, telling Perez that nothing had really happened to them, he screamed at them until they finally agreed that they had been raped. When Perez confronted the Wenatchee parents with the accusations made by their children, some described the way he questioned them. One reasonably intelligent middle-class woman said that he repeatedly asked her, "Did you have sex with him? How many times?" She could take only so much of this and reported that the detective was harassing her so much that she thought that if she only would admit the things that Perez was concurrently typing up, the charges would be so unbelievable as to be ignored. So she complied and answered, "Yeah, whatever." But this was all Perez needed.

After this housewife was arrested, her pastor came to her defense, leading Perez eventually to question him also about his own alleged abuses. When several children in his congregation and one credible middle-class parent backed up the story about sex parties in the church basement every Friday night, the pastor and his wife were also arrested. One mother immediately recanted her confession, saying that Perez had coerced it. But stories about local parents' abuse continued to come to Perez's attention and Wenatchee began to look like a cesspool of extremely deviant people. Many of their children were put into foster homes and some were sent to an Idaho mental hospital for medication and therapy.

Perez's investigation continued to grow to include even one of the Child Welfare Service caseworkers who routinely visited one of the girls placed under his care. Since this girl told him that her statements had been coerced by Perez, the caseworker filed a report with the juvenile detention officer about the detective's interview tactics. The caseworker was soon arrested and charged with witness tampering. No charges were made against him but he was subsequently fired. Since the caseworker had a five-year-old son, his name was soon added to the list of child sex abusers. Fearing that his son might be the next child seized and taken away, the caseworker fled to Canada with his family. Other caseworkers were also fired when they were bold enough to question Perez's tactics.

In the long run, ten adults were convicted in this case while another eighteen pleaded guilty to felony charges. Three others were acquitted. Charges were dropped before trial in twelve other cases. The poor, illiterate couple whose two daughters' stories started the investigation all pleaded guilty. Their sixteen-year-old son, who denied that any abuse happened in his family, was discredited and sent off to be permanently adopted. In all, four of their children were sent to foster homes and mental hospitals. Other convicted parents were sentenced to long prison terms but the pastor was acquitted at trial. One accused couple filed a civil suit against the city of Wenatchee. Other similar suits soon followed. The middle-class mother who signed a confession and then recanted, eventually pleaded guilty and served time in prison, but later had her conviction reversed.

Early in the investigation, the faculty of the University of Washington Law School, highly suspicious about the reported tactics of Detective Perez, set up an Innocence Project, based on the model developed by lawyers Barry Scheck and Peter Neufeld at the Benjamin Cardozo Law School in New York. Dozens of law faculty, local attorneys, and law students organized their own investigation into the facts of the case, including the interrogation tactics of Detective Perez. Well into their work they decided that linguistic analysis of the tactics might be useful, so they called me, along with Professor Gail Stygall of the University of Washington, to help them.

The story, briefly described above, covers only a small part of the chaos that overwhelmed the city of Wenatchee in the period from 1994 to 2000. During this time, the newly created Innocence Project unveiled information that showed that Detective Perez had lied in his reports and that many policemen, social workers, and prosecutors had withheld exculpatory evidence in the many cases they worked on and tried. The project also collected evidence of prosecutorial misconduct, perjury, and unethical behavior by judges. It was discovered that even some of the original defense attorneys did little or nothing to assist their clients, and the project also began to reveal the overzealousness of some social workers, doctors, and community members.

With no tape recordings of the interviews done by Detective Perez, the linguists' job was made difficult. Public written records, including police reports and trial transcripts of defendants and Detective Perez, were not as good as tapes, but stylistic analysis of them proved very useful, making it abundantly clear that the signed confessions were not, as Perez had testified, in the defendants' own words. Perez had said that he simply wrote down their words in a verbatim manner, but linguistic analysis of various syntactic features of both Perez and the defendants indicated otherwise—that the confession statements were written in the detective's own words, and not in the words of the defendants.

The data for linguistic analysis consisted of alleged verbatim confessions from seven of the defendants and the transcripts of their testimony at hearings and trials, including those of Doris Green. Also available was the transcript testimony of Detective Perez at hearings and trials as well as his written reports. These documents were not the usual types of evidence for which a linguist could discover conversation strategies that might be relevant to a trial. But even the reported speech in these documents revealed strong clues about how they talked.

At some points in their testimony, defendants and Perez used their memories to reconstruct various pieces of dialogue. Extremely long dialogic passages were offered in Perez's police reports. When interviewed by the media, some of the defendants also reported their conversations with Perez. Even from such indirect reports of past conversations, it appeared rather clear that Perez (and some of the social workers) had at times used the conversation strategies of ambiguity, blocking through interruption, camouflaging, ignoring "no" responses, inaccurate restatements, withholding important information, and scripting.

To anyone familiar with police reports, those written by Perez stood out as unique. The usual police jargon appeared only intermittently, if at all. The sequencing of events, which police reports conventionally try to keep straight, was not very evident when Perez wrote. In fact, the reports done by Perez come closer to the writing of a sensational pornographic magazine article. For one thing, rather than being written in the usual expository prose style, they were laced with long, racy quotations, such as his report written about what he learned from one female child (real names omitted to preserve their anonymity):

I then asked [female child] about [adult]. [Child] said, "He gave us lots of stuff. He would give me money he had with him. [Adult] used to baby-sit us. One time, he took us to the woods to go fishing for the day and he did it to me in a tent. He usually put it up my bottom and made me suck his dick. The boys were playing and not in the tent." [Child] then said, "He had a Ford truck. He took us somewhere and sent the boys off. Then he pulled a blanket over me in the front seat and made me suck his dick until stuff came out. I pretended to swallow but I did spit it out. He did this to me every time he baby-sat us. It happened about once a week for about a year. Mom and Dad knew [male adult] was doing it to me because I told her."

Perez's ability to remember long passages of conversation without benefit of a tape recorder is suspicious in itself. As noted earlier, he destroyed all his notes of the interviews with the children but even the best note taker would be not be able to recall such long passages. The reconstructed dialogue of an even longer stretch, this time with a male child, was reported by Perez as follows:

[Male child] said, "Once, [male adult] and [female adult] came into the room and brought their dog, too, in the playroom. The mattresses were on the floor and pushed together. They made me have sex with them the same as my mom did to me. [Female adult] humped me. I screwed her in front and licked her privates and sucked her boobs. She sucked my dick. [Male adult] barely did anything to me, only butt humped [female child] and licked her privates. He'd make her suck his penis. I saw it all happen. This went on for about two years." [Male child] then described another incident at his home. "Mom and Dad came up and joined in the sex. All of us were together. They had to help my mom get up the stairs. Mom, Dad, [male adult], [female adult], my brother, [male child friend] and my sister and me were there. [Brother] was humping Mom, [male child friend] was doing it to his mom at the same time. [Sister] was getting done by male adult] and Dad at the same time. I had to hump Mom and lick her privates and screw her. [Another male friend] and the dogs were watching. This happened upstairs and downstairs. Sometimes they offered us money to do it but if we said no, they did it to us anyway. Sometimes [male friend] humped [female adult], [female child] sucked [male friend's] dick, and [sister] and me had to hump each other. Then we kept going around, switching around. There were girls with girls, boys with boys, then girls with boys. It was kids with kids while the adults watched. This happened three times a month for about three years. [Adult male] taped the stuff going on."

Not only does it strain the imagination to believe that Perez could have recalled verbatim such a long discourse but, also, based on later interviews with the alleged narrators, there is no reason to believe that they would be able even to maintain complex continuous discourse involving many people and many actions. What Perez always omitted in his report were the questions he asked that led to the alleged responses by the children. Such practice is common in police reports. We can never know what type of questioning led up to these statements, or, for that matter, if they were ever made at all. If Perez had tape-recorded his interviews, we could know what really happened. Curiously, one child reported that an adult had taped some of the "stuff going on." But this was never mentioned again. One might expect Perez to have tried to obtain such a tape to prove his case.

So what conversation strategies did Perez actually use? We have very little direct evidence, but quite a bit of reported evidence, all of which he denied at hearings and trials. Virtually all of the defendants claimed that he blocked them by interrupting and shouting them down every time they tried to claim their innocence. He certainly ignored their efforts to deny his accusations. He also rejected all their efforts to recant their confessions. Perhaps more than anything else, however, the older children and the adults all said that he scripted them in what to say. Apparently he also went beyond scripting them, according to some, creating some of their statements from his own fertile imagination.

Twenty-eight people were arrested or pleaded guilty to reduced charges during the two-year investigation between 1994 and 1996. By 2000, eight of the convictions had been thrown out by the State Court of Appeals and five appeals were still pending. Eight people remained in prison serving long sentences. Perez no longer works for the Wenatchee police department and the city faces numerous civil suits for the whole sorry affair.

I report this case here, even though I have no direct evidence of the way Detective Perez abused the legal process with his conversational strategies. Stylistic analysis of the comparison of Perez's own language use with that of the defendants gave clear evidence that he did not, as he claimed, write down exactly what they said. That he induced many mentally retarded and otherwise disturbed children to make the accusations is not a tribute to effective police interrogation techniques. That he based his claims on unsubstantiated reports of what he claimed to have heard from the children is a strong warning to police interviewers to use tape recorders and to preserve their notes. That he got many illiterate, uneducated, and troubled adults to sign confessions smacks of shooting fish in a barrel.

However unprofessional, inept, and dishonest Detective Perez may have been in these cases, the legal checks and balances that one might expect were simply not at work in the system. The social workers and child-protection team workers brought into the investigation are said to have done a remarkably poor job, possibly out of incomplete or inept training but also because the case offered these departments a way to justify a larger state budget. Likewise, many of the lawyers appointed to defend the accused were said to have provided sloppy and unprofessional defenses of their clients. The Wenatchee Police Department did itself no credit by appointing Perez to a position for which he was ill-qualified and eventually proved to be incompetent. And finally, the prosecutors might have been a great deal more alert to the clear and outstanding aberrations in their cases.

14

An Undercover Policeman Uses Ambiguity, Hit and Run, Interrupting, Scripting, and Refusing to Take "No" for an Answer in a Solicitation to Murder Case: *The Crown v. Mohammed Arshad*

In the summer of 2001, the Arshads, a Pakistani family living in Scotland with three young-adult daughters, were struggling to adjust to the very different Western way of life at their new home in Dundee. In their traditional Muslim culture it was understood that the parents would arrange their daughters' marriages to suitable husbands found back in Pakistan. Any variation from this practice brought great shame on the parents and family. It was further understood that the eldest would marry first, since any variation on this practice would doom an older unmarried daughter to spinsterhood.

Mohammed Arshad was not a wealthy man. He had suffered various illnesses and had been out of work for some time. It would cost him quite a bit to fly his three daughters back to Pakistan to find husbands and he was having difficulty saving enough money to do so. His daughters were now twenty-six, twenty-four, and twenty-three, so the opportunity to arrange their marriages in the home country was growing more and more limited.

The plight of people transplanted into a different culture in a foreign context is common. In Britain, even for Muslims, the times were changing and newer practices of finding mates were evolving. Even traditional Muslim parents were becoming more liberal in their concept of marriage and courtship. Couples were now even being allowed to meet alone several times before making their decisions about mates. If this "speed date" practice seemed to work, they then met with their parents to seek parental blessing. Especially among middle-class Pakistani parents who are integrating into British life, the notion of an arranged marriage is becoming more fluid and the children are beginning to have more say about whom they will marry. But even this newer hybrid system holds onto the older tradition of the need to preserve common religious beliefs, to be from the same caste, to have an equal education level, and to have similar personal character, while the newer system continues to emphasize that marriage based on physical attraction is not good enough.

Many Pakistani parents now living in Great Britain have had to adapt to new ways, partly because the number of potential marriage partners is much smaller than in their home country. But Mohammed Arshad was not one of these. He steadfastly clung to traditional values and practices, maintaining that he would be deeply shamed if his daughters didn't follow the old ways.

Late in the summer of 2001, the Arshads got a cell-phone call from a woman saying that she was going to introduce her brother, Abdullah, as a possible suitor for Arshad's middle daughter, Insha. Arshad knew that his older daughter must marry first, but despite this, after a few more cell-phone calls, Arshad and his wife agreed to meet the young man at a public restaurant. They were not impressed with the man and they told Abdullah's family as much. He was from a different caste and was much older than their twenty-four-year-old middle daughter. But the cell-phone calls persisted through the autumn months, when the Arshads eventually learned that Insha, without their knowledge, had been secretly seeing the man. Then Abdullah himself called Arshad and reported that he and Insha had run off and gotten married, even though she was still living in Arshad's home. When confronted with this information, Insha would say nothing. Finally, she ran away, presumably to be with her new husband. Arshad was unable find out where they were, however.

Arshad was frantic. He soon got another cell-phone call, this time from Abdullah's uncle, a doctor, saying that Insha was in his "custody" and under police protection. Arshad told others about his problem and an acquaintance named Marco informed Arshad that a similar thing had happened to him once, adding that people who do that "should be dead." Marco visited with Arshad several times after that, often suggesting that he had contacts who could "sort out the problem" for him. Arshad neither agreed nor disagreed.

Not long after this, Arshad received a phone call from a man who called himself Peter, telling Arshad that Marco had contacted him about his problem. Peter convinced Arshad to meet with him at a public restaurant to discuss this. Since they had not met before, Peter suggested that they would recognize each other when Peter would ask him, "You got a problem?"

This meeting took place in late December 2001, along with a follow-up meeting a few days later. Unbeknownst to Arshad, Peter was an undercover Dundee policeman who tape-recorded both meetings. These tape-recorded conversations formed the evidence used to indict Arshad for soliciting the murder of his daughter's new husband Abdullah.

Since Arshad had no money to defend himself, a local solicitor, R. S. B. Macdonald, was appointed by the Scottish Legal Aid Board to represent him. Tape cases are not as common in the United Kingdom as they are in the United States, so Macdonald got hold of my book, *Language Crimes*, suspecting that linguistic analysis might help him better understand how to deal with these two taped conversations at trial. Macdonald believed that the alleged murder plot, if there was one, was instigated, controlled, and channeled by the police officer and that when Arshad showed unwillingness to further the conversation, the officer prevented him from doing so. Macdonald further suspected that linguistic analysis could help him show this to a jury.

Solicitor Macdonald sent me the tapes of the initial phone call and the two meetings, and I proceeded to try to determine whether or not any specific proposal was made by the policeman, and if so, whether or not it was agreed to by Arshad. I am quite familiar with the fact that undercover police often are not explicit in their representations of illegality and that the target's efforts to say "no" are sometimes blocked by the agent. It remained to be seen whether or not this was true of these tapes. After listening over and over again to the conversations, I prepared a written report of my findings and sent it to Solicitor Macdonald.

This case reveals five crucial conversational strategies used by the undercover officer in the tape-recorded conversations used against Mr. Arshad in this case, as follows:

Ambiguity and Scripting Strategies

Although I was unacquainted with the requirements of Scottish undercover law-enforcement officers about their need to represent the illegality of the enterprise as they tape-record their targets, such requirements are clear for the FBI in the United States. These guidelines were articulated by Assistant Attorney General Philip Heymann in his testimony before the House Committee on the Judiciary, and reported in the document, *FBI Undercover Operations*, 98th Congress, 2nd session, 1984. To my knowledge, there have been no further amendments to these guidelines, one of which reads as follows: "The second major safeguard followed in every undercover operation, of making clear and unambiguous to all concerned the illegal nature of any opportunity used as a decoy" (36).

One way that ambiguity occurs is when two participants in a conversation have very different schemas about the topics. Linguists refer to frames of reference, also called schemas, as the background knowledge that predisposes people to interpret their experience in a certain way. Thus, two people may hear the same words and still understand different things because of their differences in background, experience, expectations, and knowledge.

It is apparent in these conversations that Arshad and the officer frequently did not share the same frame of reference. This difference is partially revealed in the topics they introduced and recycled. The officer's single conversational agenda, as revealed by the topics he introduced, was to capture a crime on tape. Arshad's primary conversational agenda, as revealed by the topics he introduced, was to get his daughter back, in order to avoid the family shame resulting from her running off and marrying Abdullah. These different agendas are clearly revealed throughout the taped conversations.

From Arshad's undisputed precognition statement, we learn that the stimulus for the meeting with the officer came from Arshad's friend, Marco, who, without Arshad's knowledge or agreement, had arranged for the undercover officer to seek out and meet with Arshad. It is important to note that there is nothing in the evidence showing that Arshad had asked Marco to find a hit man for him. It is also important to note who pursued whom in this case. Arshad evidenced surprise in his conversations with the undercover officer. That Arshad was uncertain about how this man could help him is apparent in the two phone calls setting up their eventual meeting, neither of which specified what the caller meant when he said he could help Arshad with his "wee problem" and what he meant by "sort it out." From the outset, the two men had different frames of reference.

Based on their first meeting, on December 27, Peter's vague and ambiguous references to helping Arshad with his problem only exacerbated the differences in their frames of reference. The officer denied that Marco had told him what the "problem" was, so Arshad identified his problem from his own frame of reference:

> "My daughter has been seeing someone without my knowledge and they went and got married."
>
> * * *
>
> "This guy is not letting her speak to me."
>
> * * *
>
> "I get threatened by it."

After stating his problem, Arshad then listed some of the things he wanted to see happen:

> "I want to have him not out of the picture, still in the picture, but not in a moveable way."
>
> * * *
>
> "I want him removed so nobody knows where he is."
>
> * * *
>
> "He's got to be removed from this earth."
>
> * * *
>
> "But the body has to be seen by the parents or whoever but he does not exist any longer."

The order of Arshad's list suggests his own agenda and priorities: his missing daughter and the threat this posed to him being paramount. Only after he lists these does Arshad describe what he "wants" (to remove the man from this earth).

One issue here is what Arshad means by "out of the picture, still in the picture, but not in a moveable way," "removed from this earth," "does not exist any longer," and his reference to "the body." The officer's frame of reference apparently is that Arshad wants to have Abdullah killed, even though Arshad had not specifically said this.

It also should be noted that what a person "wants" is not the same thing as a directive to someone else to do anything to help accomplish such wants. Apparently recognizing that Arshad had still not given him a directive, the officer then asked how Arshad wanted this accomplished. Arshad listed some methods for finding Abdullah, but again he did not give the officer any directives. His frame of reference about what needed to be done is clear from the following summary of his talk:

- the need to locate the man;
- the way would be first doing "something" to the family;
- getting photographs of him;
- finding the address of the family.

Apparently recognizing that Arshad had still not given him a directive to do a killing, the officer then backed up a bit and asked, "Okay, what, what sort of injury are you thinking to his family?" Note that by using the word, "injury," the officer elevated Arshad's "doing *something* to the family" to "*injuring* the family." Building on this, the officer then suggested, "Are you thinking of an accident or something else?" to which Arshad replied, "Make it look like a racist attack," words that do not necessarily require personal injury and do not denote killing.

Arshad returned to his view of the problem, again illustrating his frame of reference:

- Abdullah's family wouldn't let him speak to his daughter;
- they wouldn't put the phone to her ear;
- they said she didn't want to speak with him;
- when from a distance Arshad heard his daughter say "no," Arshad didn't know if this meant "no" to speaking with him or "no" to Abdullah;
- Arshad thought that his daughter was very frightened about this.

Again, apparently recognizing that Arshad had still not given him a directive to kill anyone, the officer continued to try to elicit this, asking more directly, "What do you want to happen to him then?" To this Arshad replied, "He has got to go." The officer apparently interpreted this as, "You want him to die," but after Peter requested clarification, Arshad stuck with his words, repeating "He's got to go." At issue in this case is what "got to go" meant to Arshad. Although it is clear what "got to go" meant in officer Peter's frame of reference, it is not explicitly clear that Arshad intended the same meaning.

Still failing to elicit the clear directive to kill that he was after, the officer's conversational strategy was then to ask, "How do you want this done then?" Arshad gave no useful response. In fact, there was a thirteen-second pause with no response at all from Arshad, after which the officer probed again, "What have you thought?" Undaunted, the officer then recycled Arshad's earlier use of the word, "body," explaining that there is an additional problem if the man simply disappears. Here the officer began to teach Arshad that if his daughter's new husband was not found, his daughter would undoubtedly wonder where he was and simply wait for him. In short, she would not come back home to Arshad. The passage shows that Arshad admitted that he had not thought his actions through and that the officer was scripting Arshad to consider something that he had hitherto not expressed.

The more Arshad described his problem, the more openly agitated he became. He even told the officer that he had once considered getting a gun with a silencer, although he did not say what he would do with it. Since this still did not constitute a directive to the officer to kill anyone, the officer returned to Arshad's original list, focusing on the need to first find the man. The officer volunteered to do this for him. Arshad told the officer about his own plan for finding his daughter's husband, to which the officer asked: "Is that not why you're talking to me?" Obviously Arshad's plan to do the work of finding the man by himself still did not constitute a request for the officer to do anything. If the officer were to elicit a directive to kill someone, he first needed to take over from Arshad the initial investigatory work of locating Abdullah. So he volunteered, "I think you leave that to me."

Up to the time when Peter asked, "Are you sure you want this done?" the conversational topic had been only to locate Insha's new husband. Arshad's response to this question, "I am two hundred percent sure," grammatically can only mean that he's sure that now he is beginning to accept the officer's offer to help find Abdullah. But to this point there had still been no directive to kill anyone. The officer then introduced the price for doing "this," noting that it was a "big thing":

Peter: This thing we're talking about is a big thing.
Arshad: I've got to know what sort of a figure it is so I know if I can afford it or not.

Arshad pointed out that his friend Marco had told him "it" would cost him about five hundred pounds. Since "it" was not specified, at issue here is what the five hundred pounds was to pay for. To this point there had still been no directive to kill anyone. There had been only talk about locating Insha's husband. Based on the going rate for solicitation to murder cases in the United States at least, five hundred pounds would be far below the acceptable figure. This rate is more consistent with the cost of doing investigative work and there is no reason to believe that a hit would be this inexpensive in Scotland.

So what did Arshad think he was paying for? The discussion about the cost continued. The officer dropped hints about not wanting to attract police attention and he continued to use ambiguous and unspecific terms such as "this," "the deal," "something that's done," and finally, "we have to find them and we have to do that side of it then we have to carry it out." This last expression was apparently the officer's rather inexplicit effort to separate the investigative finding job from a killing job. That Arshad did not recognize this effort was clear from his next statement, which was still focused on locating Abdullah and his family but silent about having anybody killed.

The officer next gave his own directive to Arshad, "Don't do anything just now . . . leave that with me." The question here is what the officer meant by his directive to not do anything just now as well as what "that" referred to. Since Arshad appeared to be agreeing to let the officer do the investigating, there is reason to believe that Arshad interpreted these words to mean just that. The officer may have thought that he had communicated the meaning of "don't do the killing just now" but there is no grammatical or contextual discourse support for such an interpretation.

The topic of payment for services then came up again and the officer's request of "five K" was met with Arshad's clear rejection: "Thanks for your time anyway." Eventually the officer suggested reducing his price to one thousand pounds, still more consistent with the price of an investigation than a hit. The officer requested an advance of two hundred pounds, to which Arshad agreed, but the participants' different frames of reference led them to different interpretations of what it was for.

Arshad then said that he'd do "it" himself if the officer doesn't. What does Arshad's "it" mean here? Note that the consistent ongoing topic had been about how to locate Abdullah and his family. Arshad finally agreed to pay two hundred down for the officer to do this (note that the officer still had not elicited Arshad's explicit directive to do any killing). The officer agreed that Arshad wouldn't have to pay until he's "got the goods." Then Arshad replied, "It will be done even if I have to do it, no matter if I get caught or not, it will be done either way." Arshad's grammatical reference to "it" here appears to be that of locating Arshad's family.

At this point the officer appeared to fear that he was losing this job, almost frantically saying, "Okay, well I can help you here. I can help you." The officer added the guilt tactic, urging Arshad not to go to the police out of guilt. This apparently hit a cultural nerve for Arshad. He replied that he didn't feel guilty and said that if anybody had guilt, it should be Abdullah. Arshad said that he wouldn't feel guilt "even if I've got to kill her. . . . I've raised her for twenty-four years and then I get this." At this point, Arshad's intonation indicated that he was in a highly emotional state. Noteworthy is that this utterance began with a conditional "if" clause, which cannot be equated with a directive or, for that matter, even a prediction.

About his daughter's husband, Arshad added, "I am very under stress, maybe I cannot speak very clearly due to circumstances." He then said, "I have many things on my mind but to bring him, stab, stab the bastard—" (unfinished sentence). Things on Arshad's mind cannot be equated with what he will actually do. He was expressing his utter contempt for his daughter's new husband in words that are common in many conflict-talk situations. Arshad's use of "but" in this sentence also bears attention. There are several meanings of "but." It can be a contraster (indicating that something different will follow). It can be an excluder (except for). It is also possible that it started a new contrastive clause that was never finished here (possibly "but I could never do that").

The officer then recycled what his work for Arshad would cost, and Arshad replied, "I want to work it out. Obviously maybe I can afford this. Obviously somebody else has got to get the job and they're looking for something more which unfortunately I cannot afford and though I am sorry." Hearing this unclear statement, the officer appeared to be confused and asked for clarification:

> *Peter:* What are you saying? What are you saying? What's your top line? A grand?
> *Arshad:* That, that would be it.

But still at issue was what the "grand" was for. Arshad had given no directive for the officer to kill anyone. There had only been considerable talk about the officer trying to locate Abdullah and his family. The price for doing this fell within the normal range of an investigation, but outside the normal range of a hit. Arshad agreed to give the officer two hundred pounds up front, once he was able to borrow the money.

The extent to which the undercover officer in the Arshad case failed to be clear and unambiguous in his representation of what he was proposing to Arshad can be seen in his following statements for which the terms, "something," "it," "problem," "job," "this," "that," "help," "act," "things," "got," "happen," and "work" had no previously defined references (page numbers of the transcript are included to show the temporal progression):

December 24 Call

p. 1	you may need a bit of help on *something*
p. 2	I think I should be able to help you on *this*.
p. 2	I should be able to sort this wee problem out for you
p. 3	and hopefully we'll be able to *sort it out* then

December 27 Meeting

p. 2	tell me about your *problem*
p. 2	I'm here to *help you*
p. 3	I can do *something* for you
p. 3	is there anybody else doing *this same job* for you?
p. 4	tell me what your *problem* is
p. 4	I should be able to *sort it out* for you
p. 4	you've got the *problem* and we'll *sort it out*
p. 5	Well, I don't specifically know what your *problem* is
p. 5	I can look at *it* and do *something* for you

AMBIGUITY IN A SOLICITATION TO MURDER CASE

p. 5	the least people that know what your *problem* is . . .
p. 5	if *this* is what I think *it* is
p. 5	treat *it* as a business venture
p. 6	who's got the *problem*
p. 6	it's your *problem* then
p. 6	and we do *this* deal together
p. 7	are you sure you want to go through with *this*?
p. 7	Is *it* his *problem* or is it your *problem*?
p. 8	Do you want to tell me what your *problem* is?
p. 9	And what are your thoughts on how *this* should be done?
p. 10	How soon do you want *this* to take place?
p. 10	change your mind about *this*?
p. 16	Okay, we can work *this* out. We can work *this* out.
p. 16	We can work *this* out.
p. 17	I can do *some work* myself
p. 18	We can have a look and *take it from there*
p. 19	start to open *this* up
p. 19	I think you leave *that* to me
p. 19	I can *sort something out*, alright
p. 20	You're 200 percent sure you want *this* done?
p. 20	*This thing* we're talking about is a big *thing*.
p. 21	There's a lot of planning needs to be done in to *this*
p. 22	What's you limit on *this*?
p. 22	When *this* is done *it's* gonna be over.
p. 22	but *the deal* is done and we won't see you again
p. 23	So I want *this* to be *something* that's done and then *it's* finished.
p. 23	*it's* business . . . I have to do *that*
p. 23	and *this* is done
p. 23	we have to do that side of *it* and then we have to carry *it* out
p. 24	what somebody's willing to pay for *it*
p. 24	what somebody's willing to pay for *it*
p. 25	There's still a lot of work to be done on *it*
p. 26	*this* isn't an easy *job*
p. 26	*it's* only worth what *it's* worth to whoever
p. 26	Do you want *this* done?
p. 27	and do these things and keep you away from *it*
p. 27	to have a look at *these things*
p. 27	*this* is a slightly different type of business
p. 27	You would do *it* yourself?
p. 28	Okay, well I can *help* you here, I can *help* you
p. 28	if you give me the job, I'll do *the job* for you
p. 28	only us know about *it* . . . which is why *it* works
p. 31	*it's* hurting you *this*, *this thing* is hurting you

p. 31	How much is *it* worth?
p. 31	Is *it* worth that much?
p. 31	*it's* only worth what somebody can pay
p. 35	Okay, you're still sure, you're sure about *this*?
p. 38	Now one last time, are you sure about *this*?

December 28 Meeting

p. 3	have you been having *a think*?
p. 14	the next contact you have with me is when *this* is done
p. 15	I'm gonna *carry out an act* that might bring them all to the house
p. 16	will take the form of *a physical attack* to get them to come
p. 16	are you still quite happy about *hurting* him?
p. 17	once I've *got* him I'm gonna leave
p. 17	*take him out*, okay
p. 18	you'll know that *this is being done* . . .
p. 19	Are you happy for *what's gonna happen*?
p. 19	*something's* only worth what *it's* worth
p. 20	nobody else knows *it* will be done
p. 20	*This* will be done. *This* is why I am here.
p. 20	you might have *some work* in the future?
p. 22	I'm gonna be starting on *this* straight away

The above instances show that there were many opportunities for the officer to be explicit, clear, and unambiguous about the illegal nature of the opportunity he wished to represent. Instead, he resorted to vagueness and ambiguity. Whenever there is vagueness and ambiguity in language, there is always a danger that the respondent will not understand the intended message. When the participants have different frames of reference, the chances of miscommunication only expand. It is common for law enforcement officers who are accused of being ambiguous or vague to defend such behavior by saying that if they had been clear and explicit, the target would have walked away. But the possibility of ensnaring an innocent person is precisely the reason why they should be unambiguous. The desire to win, so deeply grounded in most humans, should not overcome the primary need to be fair.

A clear and explicit representation of one's goals leads to clear and explicit responses. If the target understands the words differently, there is no agreement. Examples of how it would have been easy for the officer to have been explicit include: "I'm here to do the hit for you," "leave the killing to me," and "are you sure that you want me to kill him for you?" The officer did not do this in the phone call or in the December 27 meeting.

At the second meeting on December 28, perhaps recognizing this continuing ambiguity, the officer then recycled a word used by Arshad in the meeting the day before, "body." This was perhaps the most difficult reference for Arshad to overcome in his case:

> *Peter*: Okay. Again, you said yesterday you would prefer that the body be found, you know, do you still go with that?
> *Arshad*: This way if the body's found obviously everybody knows.
> *Peter*: Uh-huh.
> *Arshad*: Dead.
> *Peter*: Okay.
> *Arshad*: My daughter might think that he's dead. She might just come back. If she doesn't know, he's disappeared instead, she might think he coming back in a week's time, he out of the country or is he where. She might wait for him, no idea—
> *Peter*: (*interrupting*) Okay, so it would be better if the body was found?
> *Arshad*: If the body is found, obviously I'm thinking on your part as well. If the body was found as you say, the postmortem and all this, what sort of, what would that bring out?
> *Peter*: You understand that?

However troublesome this passage was for Arshad, it also must be seen in relationship to the officer's earlier teaching of Arshad. It shows how Arshad compliantly reflected the scripting that the officer had given Arshad on the previous day, after Arshad had talked about his wish for the husband to disappear, of being "removed from this earth." Here Arshad pointed out that it was the officer who had explained to him the advantages of having a body, dutifully repeating this alleged advantage. The major significance of this passage is that even though Arshad now acknowledged the advantage of there being a body to find, the officer had still not elicited an explicit agreement from Arshad to kill anyone.

The officer then guided the discussion to a possible "racist attack" on the family members as a method to be used, noting that once the location was established, it was a way of drawing out Insha's husband. To accomplish this, the officer first suggested that he might start a fire. Arshad rejected this since it might implicate his younger brother, who previously had mentioned something to the family about "firing" them out of their house.

The officer then suggested, "maybe a physical attack" on the family. He brought up the doctor's children and Arshad explained why he had to reject this idea, mentioning that he himself had once considered abducting them for a few days, but abandoned it as a very bad idea.

Arshad suggested a third method: "damaging the doctor, the husband, or the sister." At the completion of this idea the officer said:

> *Peter*: Right, when I leave here, yeah, the next contact, yeah, you have with me is when *this* is done.
> *Arshad*: Right.
> *Peter*: . . . after that if I've not been successful in tracing them I'm gonna carry out an act that might bring them all to the house, and as you said, it could be an injury to the doctor or an injury to the daughters, okay, and that may take the form of a racist incident.

Arshad again objected to bringing any harm to the daughters, but agreed that the doctor's sister could be targeted for "an injury." In this segment, the officer agreed to create a type of racist incident that might harm the doctor or his sister as a way of drawing out Insha's new husband. The topic for the preceding colloquy was about this, but not about killing anyone. The officer's use of "when this is done" grammatically refers to the proposed racist event, not to a killing. Any contract they may have made, thus far at least, can only be interpreted in this way. That even the officer understood this is clear from his next statement: "That happening will take the form of a racist attack to get them to come back to have sympathy with them."

Once again, the officer checked to see if Arshad was happy with this idea, but once again he tried to tie it back to killing Insha's husband. He asked, "Are you still quite happy, I mean you're saying that, are you still quite happy about hurting him?" This is typically ambiguous, for the "him" grammatically refers to the doctor, not to the husband, and is associated with the proposed racist attack on the family. That Arshad understands "him" to mean the doctor is seen in his response, "Yes, oh fuck, oh fuck, it's just his kids (*inaudible*)." Since only the doctor had kids, the officer's "him" is understood to be the doctor.

Arshad then elaborated about the people who were involved with his problem—the doctor, his wife, and whoever else, noting that he wanted to find out who any other witnesses at his daughter's marriage to Abdullah might be, since they might shed light on whether or not their alleged marriage actually ever took place. To this the officer interrupted and asked for clarification: "So wait, wait a minute here, so what are you contracting me for even?" This question reveals that even the officer is not clear about the contract they were trying to make. His own ambiguity had contributed to this greatly and it is also the case that Arshad had been less than clear about it himself. So Arshad then tried to clarify:

> *Arshad*: This is only for the doctor or the family, getting, cutting them or whatever to bring him back and getting rid of him at this present moment . . . the other one which is, that's a later stage. I cannot offer . . . something for that as well.

This was perhaps the clearest statement Arshad had made about his proposed contract with the officer. Arshad pointed out that his problem has two stages. The first stage, for which he was agreeing to the officer's offer to help, was to find the family and do some sort of harm ("cutting" is suggested here) to an unspecified member, excluding the children. The second stage, which he identified here as "the other one" was to come later, if at all. This proposed contract with the officer cannot be for the killing since Arshad pointed out that he "cannot offer" for that one. This had been clearly stated in the December 27 conversation, when Arshad said several times that he could not afford it.

Despite this clarification by Arshad, the officer then said, rather ambiguously again:

> *Peter*: Him I'm gonna leave, take him out, okay, and then I'm gonna be looking for my payment.
> *Arshad*: By all means, yes.

The question here is what the officer meant and what Arshad understood. In light of their preceding exchanges, "Him I'm gonna leave" appears to mean that the officer was not going to do the second possible stage, the killing of Abdullah. But the officer's following words, "take him out," remain cleverly ambiguous. Did the officer mean that he was going to do the second stage, to kill the husband? That is one possible meaning. But it also can mean, "take the husband-killing part out of this job." The officer left it dangling ambiguously, quickly changing the topic back to the need for payment (an example of the "hit-and-run strategy"). Arshad's response above grammatically refers to the payment. In linguistics, the "recency principle" states that when multiple propositions are made, the response is normally to the last or most recent one. This logic indicates that Arshad's "by all means, yes" response is to the payment.

From this point on, the officer continued to be ambiguous about what he would do, using expressions such as "You'll know that *this* is being done," and "are you happy with *that*," with no specific references to identify the meaning of "this" and "that."

Near the very end, the officer, perhaps recognizing his own previous consistently ambiguous representations, finally used the "kill" word: "Are you sure you want me to kill him?" Arshad answers, "Too damn right, yeah." This sounds bad, but again, wanting it is not the same thing as contracting for it or doing it. In any case, a different contract had been established by now—for an investigation and doing some sort of racist attack on the doctor's family in order to draw Insha's new husband to their home. As much as Arshad would like to see the husband dead, he had been clear that he couldn't afford that job. Arshad said, in fact, "I might have to if we are not successful."

The December 28 conversation concluded with what appears to be the payment of the advance to the officer, followed by Arshad's arrest.

The Hit-and-Run Strategy

Perhaps recognizing that he had been ambiguous and unclear in the December 27 meeting, the officer tried to be clearer in the meeting on December 28. His approach is to remind Arshad about what he had said the previous day, when Arshad said that he would "shoot him" himself if he had to:

> *Peter*: I've been thinking what you said to me yesterday and I'm thinking that you mentioned that you would shoot him yourself.

> *Arshad:* If I get the chance if nobody else can do it . . . yes I would.
> *Peter:* Okay, so that's what I'm gonna do, okay? Now do you have any preference the way you want that done? What type of firearm's used?
> *Arshad:* Sorry?
> *Peter:* What type of gun is used? What type of firearm is used?
> *Arshad:* I don't care about that.

Note how the officer used the hit-and-run conversational strategy here. He first recycled Arshad's word, "shoot," then volunteered to do it for Arshad. Then the officer shifted the topic very quickly, before Arshad had a chance to reply, asking what type of firearm to use. Arshad was confused and requested clarification. The officer stayed on the firearm topic and Arshad answered that he doesn't care about that. But the damage had been carefully done.

To recapitulate at this point, whatever "contract" they had was for the officer to carry out investigative work, finding the family and exposing Insha's new husband. The payment, as explained in the December 27 meeting, was one thousand pounds for this effort. This clearly wasn't enough for the police. They were after the clear agreement to commit murder, which the officer still hadn't elicited from Arshad.

The question here is whether the intended product of the officer's hit-and-run strategy was actually understood by Arshad. His request for clarification suggested strongly that it was not, even when Arshad said, "The damage is that I just want him dead." Wanting him dead and agreeing to a contract killing are not the same things. Arshad did not say explicitly, "Yes I want him dead and I agree that you should kill him," or, alternatively, "I want you to kill him for me." Explicitness is not only a requirement for the undercover officer, it is also a requirement for the target. Without explicitness, we are left with only guesswork and inference, which works well neither for the defense nor the prosecution.

Not Taking "No" for an Answer Strategy

In the December 27 conversation, Arshad rambled from topic to topic, not making it explicitly clear what, if anything, he might want the officer to do for him. When the officer brought up payment, Arshad made it clear that he could afford only one thousand pounds. The officer responded that this was not enough. He wanted "five K." At this point, Arshad began a series of comments that functionally told the officer, "no."

> *Arshad*: Oh well, that will be straightforward then now, just beating around the bush. I don't have that.
> *Peter*: You haven't got that money?
> *Arshad*: I wouldn't be able to. Too much.
> (*forty-five-second pause*)
> *Arshad*: Thanks for your time anyway.

The officer did not take this dismissal as the end of the conversation, however. He then suggested a lower amount, a thousand pounds, to which Arshad replied in a way that also discouraged further discussion:

> *Arshad*: There's no question that price I can't afford. There is no way I can get that. It was worth coming but you've got to understand. I'm a working man.

The officer still did not quit.

> *Peter*: What are you willing to pay?
> *Arshad*: It was just what I can afford but I can't afford —
> *Peter*: You can't afford that but what can you afford?
> *Arshad*: A thousand. All I can afford is that. You understand? Maybe that's not what a better thing to do on your part but I'd still like to thank you for coming.

Inconsistently, Arshad first seemed to agree to pay a thousand, then once again thanked him for coming (a conversational pre-close), indicating that he believed the conversation was over, still another functional "no." The officer again did not take "no" for an answer. Next, he suggested a token advance of money up front. Arshad then said that he might have to do "it" himself:

> *Arshad*: . . . it will be done even if I have to do it, no matter if I get caught or not.
> *Peter*: You would do it yourself?
> *Arshad*: I will do it myself. I will do it myself . . . no matter how long it would take . . . I am willing to do it and I will do it, no matter what happens, I will do it. Maybe it takes me six months. Maybe it'll take me a year. I will do it.

Again, the officer did not take this as a "no," but instead continued to try to elicit Arshad's acceptance:

> *Peter*: Okay, well I can help you here. I can help you.
> *Arshad*: Yeah, I appreciate that you will come. But the only thing about it is I don't have much to go around.

Here Arshad was again functionally saying "no," but the officer continued to offer his service just the same:

> *Peter*: . . . If you give the job, I'll do the job for you.

The issue for law enforcement is essentially, "How many times does a target need to indicate 'no' for the officer to accept this and back off?" To continue pursuit after the target has backed off actually encourages a crime to take place, in the same way that a used-car salesperson continues to pursue a sale even though the customer has refused to purchase a car. But although the techniques are similar, there is an obvious crucial difference between a salesperson pursuing the purchase of a used car and a law officer pursuing or inducing the commission of a crime.

The Interruption Strategy

Each of the following utterances by Arshad was interrupted by the officer. When a person is interrupted in midutterance, we can never know what the rest of the utterance might have revealed. In undercover operations, interrupting is particularly troublesome, since the taped language is the only evidence we have. Good undercover officers avoid interrupting targets since the best bits of evidence against them are self-generated statements of guilt. Interrupting the target also invites the criticism of trying to block potentially exculpatory statements. Since the statements are interrupted, however, we can never know whether they would have been inculpatory or exculpatory. The dash at the end of the utterances cited below indicates the point of interruption. The following are examples of Arshad being interrupted, all from the meeting tapes (again, transcript page numbers are included to show progression):

December 27 Meeting

p. 2	Mm-mm. Well, obviously the person—
p. 7	He's been with me right from the start so it's uh—
p. 10	I will have to obtain photographs to—
p. 12	But his sister, brother-in-law, home where he—
p. 17	. . . we have a little intelligence that, uh—
p. 20	That again now—
p. 21	I don't know. I've not had the—
p. 21	I had an offer for—
p. 25	Obviously I can't. This is the thing which your—
p. 25	I was just what I can afford but I can't afford—
p. 26	Yeah, it's true but—
p. 26	Well, business is as you know—
p. 27	In business I should say until the goods are there—
p. 28	Will the job, uh—

December 28 Meeting

p. 7	I think it would be reading glasses, ordinary—
p. 13	That time him being a doctor, obviously his clinic or whatever—
p. 15	I've never seen her, by the sound of her over the phone with three children—
p. 16	. . . the only way I was thinking was because they would come back if they are abducted or terror, hurting a youngster is not nice but, uh—
p. 16	. . . I am still finding out who the witnesses are—

Conclusions

The five conversational strategies used by the undercover officer in this case supported Solicitor Macdonald's suspicion that the plot to kill

Arshad's daughter's new husband was instigated, controlled, and channeled by Peter, the undercover police officer. Linguistic analysis of the above mentioned conversations indicates that the undercover officer:

- failed to elicit from Arshad a directive to kill anyone;
- was vague and ambiguous in his representation of illegality;
- tried to make it look like they agreed upon contract to determine the location of the place where his daughter had been hidden and, later, to create the appearance of a "racial attack" that would bring his daughter and her husband back to Arshad's family home, was instead a contract to have the daughter's husband murdered;
- refused to accept Arshad's repeated functional "no" responses to his offer to kill, but kept on trying to elicit agreement anyway;
- scripted Arshad to consider the need for a dead body;
- used conversation strategies that prevented Arshad from responding fully and appropriately, including the "hit-and-run" strategy and the strategy of interrupting him at potentially important points.

It was unfortunate that on the date the trial was scheduled, I was in the hospital having surgery. Solicitor Macdonald tried in vain to get a delay in the trial. The outcome of the short trial was equally unfortunate for Arshad, who was convicted of soliciting murder and sentenced to seven years in prison. His conviction was appealed, however, based partially on the fact that Macdonald was not able to call the linguistic expert witness, and, if the appeal succeeds, there may be a retrial ahead.

15

Manipulating the Tape, Interrupting, Inaccurate Restatements, and Scripting in a Murder Case: Florida v. Jerry Townsend

In 1978 a number of unsolved murders of young female prostitutes took place in the area of Fort Lauderdale and Miami, Florida. When the Dade County police questioned a mentally weak drifter named Jerry Townsend about the killings, he clearly and willingly admitted to five of them. Since the police were curious about whether Townsend was also responsible for their other unsolved murder cases, they interrogated him about this for five days between September 6, and September 10, 1979.

Only four hours of the interrogations were tape-recorded during this entire period. Much of the time was spent driving Townsend around and trying to locate the crime scenes. During this time the tape recorder was turned off, then back on many times during the recorded interrogations. In fourteen of these interrogations, the police made no mention that it was turned off or on. Electronic methods exist for determining such off/on signatures, but in most cases such analysis was not even necessary, as the following transcript evidence itself indicates:

> *Townsend*: Uh-huh, that's (*tape clicks off, then on*) walk down about one block, come up through there.
> *Townsend*: Uh-huh. That's (*clicking sound*) walk down about one block, come up through there.

The police transcript of this makes no mention of an off/on signature but simply records it as continuous speech.

It was not only the clicking sound on the tape and the garbled discourse continuity that gave clues to the off/on signature. Clear changes in background noise also supported this. A dog could be heard barking for about a minute up to Townsend's first, "that's." At his next transcribed word the barking suddenly stopped. There was also a noticeable change in volume between his softly spoken "Uh-huh, that's" and the much louder volume of the rest of his utterance, also suggesting a time lapse during which the recorder was turned off, then back on.

Other signs of police manipulation of the tapes include the sudden topic shifts that occur frequently. For example, at one point during the taping on September 10, the ongoing topic was an argument between one of the detectives and Townsend about whether the detective had manipulated Townsend into talking with the Fort Lauderdale police. The tape is cut off in the middle of one of Townsend's sentences. When it comes back on, the topic is about something very different—three girls in Tampa. On other occasions, the tape is turned back on with Townsend answering a question that was not recorded on the tape. After one of the off/on breaks, this one actually announced by the detective, the tape comes back on with Townsend saying:

Townsend: I mean seventy-seven.

We can never know what question Townsend was answering here.

Other examples of the way the detectives manipulated the tape recording follow. In order for readers to understand Townsend's language, it should be pointed out that in his own private and offbeat style of speech, "I committed suicide on her" meant "I killed her," and "I took five minutes of her time" meant "I had sexual intercourse with her."

During those four tape-recorded hours, it was clear that whenever Townsend got the answers wrong (from the detectives' perspective at least), the tape was turned off for an unknown length of time. When it was turned back on, Townsend corrected his earlier statement and offered the facts that correctly fit the details of the crime, as the following example shows:

Townsend: It was a black girl in a white Stingray.

(tape turned off, then back on)
Townsend: It was a white girl in a white Stingray.

In the interrogation on September 6, after telling the detectives that he had killed a woman with a piece of wire, one of the detectives asked him what he did with her clothes, to which Townsend answered:

Townsend: Well, those short pants. I took the pants and her blouse and just got rid of the whole thing.
Detective: Jerry, I think you're getting a little confused.
(tape turned off, then back on)
Townsend: And the time I got through with five minutes of her time, that's when I commit suicide.

Like Townsend's response to an unknown question noted earlier ("I mean seventy-seven"), we cannot know to what question this response was made. We can't know how long the recorder was turned off or what went on during that interval.

Another equally egregious example of manipulation of the tape recording is the following:

Detective: How did you kill her?
Townsend: With her bra.
(tape turned off, then back on)
Detective: Okay. And you still left the sock in her mouth, is that right?

We cannot know what happened during the time that the tape was turned off, but to that point on the tape, there had been no mention of a sock being in the victim's mouth. Note that the detective used the definite article, "the," before "sock" rather than the indefinite article, "a." Since the detective used the definite article, "the," which presupposes a previously defined reference, it is reasonable to suspect that he and Townsend had been discussing that sock during the time when the tape was not running. The word, "still," also used by the detective, supports the same suspicion. "Still" presupposes that something about socks had been already been said while the tape was not running.

After Townsend had admitted killing several prostitutes, the detective wanted to know if there were still more women he had killed:

> *Detective*: But it's up to you whether you go on with anyone else of not.
> *Townsend*: No, I—
> *(tape turned off, then back on)*
> *Detective*: Right here, tell me straight out the truth about those three girls that were shot in Tampa.

There had been no previous mention on tape of "those three girls that were shot in Tampa." The detective's own word, "those," strongly suggests that this topic was introduced while the tape was turned off. Townsend had said "no" when asked about "anyone else," and was starting to say something else, beginning with "I," but his apparent negative explanation was interrupted by the detective before it could be finished. Again, we can never know what went on during the time the tape was not running, but it is not difficult to believe that the detective's interruption indicated that he had some more unsolved murders that he wanted to clear up, whether or not Townsend had mentioned them earlier.

When interviewers put words into the suspects' mouths, they are actually scripting the evidence, a form of contamination that everyone agrees has no place in the interview process, but especially in a case of a man with mental difficulties. The Miami psychologist who examined Townsend for the defense spent five hours with him administering intelligence tests, Rorschach tests, the Bender-Gestalt tests and other diagnostic instruments. He reported that Townsend showed a "low level of mental functioning and/or brain damage." Townsend's drawing of a human figure was diagnosed as that of a three- to four-year-old. His reading was second-grade level. The psychologist said that Townsend's tests indicated a level of mental retardation. Townsend scored at the first-grade level on arithmetic. His Wechsler and Rorschach scores were at the level of a mentally retarded person. Overall, he was said to function at the level of a seven- or eight-year-old child.

A second psychologist verified the conclusions of the first one, additionally concluding that the suspect was not competent to understand the rational and factual proceedings against him: "His intellectual capacities are so limited that one cannot, with any confidence, accept any actual statement that he may have made, particularly if it has any reference to time or place or names or any details of even an elementary nature." This psychological evaluation of Townsend also reported that he functioned at the level of a six- or seven-year-old. A third psychologist verified the findings of the other two and called Townsend mentally retarded. Not surprisingly, the prosecution countered with its own psychological evaluation that claimed that Townsend had an IQ of "fifty-one or so" but that he functioned at the level of a nineteen-year-old. The prosecution's psychologist, who was not licensed and did not hold a doctorate, was ruled by the judge to not be an expert. Nevertheless, for some reason he was allowed to testify. Even more curiously, since he was not deemed to be an expert, the defense attorney was not permitted to cross-examine him. Outsiders to the workings of the law may find the Court's ruling here truly amazing.

Admittedly, it is very difficult for the police to interrogate a mentally retarded man, especially one who psychologists on both sides admitted had trouble with specifics of time, place, and names. When Townsend tried to be specific about such things, he was often self-contradictory and inconsistent. He would say that he didn't know a woman's name, then later identify her as Darlene, and even later as someone else. At one point, he admitted to choking all five girls at a baseball park, then later said that no baseball park was involved and that all five were killed in different places. Nevertheless, Townsend was convicted of nine murders in 1980 on the strength of his purported confessions.

Jerry Townsend was clearly a suggestible sitting duck for the detectives. The details he gave the police clearly contradicted crime-scene evidence. When he contradicted himself, he was fed details by the questions the police asked him. He said that he covered one body with a cardboard box after it was discovered with a tarp over it. He told police that he beat one woman, but no signs of trauma were found on her body. He called one victim "a tall broad," but she was only five foot four. As one current Miami investigator put it, "It's almost like they (the detectives) had blinders on. The signs were there. Townsend was contracting himself" ("Townsend Confessions at Odds with Evidence Review of Dade Deaths Shows Red Flags," by Amy Driscoll and Manny Garcia, *Miami Herald,* May 27, 2001, A1).

It is rare for any police department to have policies that deal with the custodial interrogation of suspects who are mentally retarded. But the story doesn't end here. In June 2001, Jerry Townsend was acquitted of the crimes to which he confessed—after serving twenty-two years in prison—when DNA evidence preserved from the original crime scene proved that the killer was not Townsend. In reviewing the tape recordings, even the Broward County sheriff allowed for the possibility that the detectives led Townsend intellectually because he was so compliant and ready to tell them what they wanted to hear. The way the detectives used the language strategies of manipulating what was on the tape, interrupting Townsend at crucial moments, inaccurately restating what Townsend had said, and scripting him to say things that would show his guilt, all contributed to this legal fiasco.

PART IV

Conversational Strategies as Evidence

The previous chapters have illustrated how different conversational strategies were used by undercover cooperating witnesses and agents in twelve different criminal cases. In each case, the tape recordings constituted the major evidence, showing how law enforcement's use of these conversational strategies exerted power over their targets. This chapter identifies the extent to which the strategies are used, why they are so powerful, and what can and cannot be done about such evidence. It takes the form of eight questions about these issues.

16

Eight Questions about the Power of Conversational Strategies in Undercover Police Investigations

This book has focused on the way law enforcement used eleven conversational strategies to overpower targets in undercover criminal cases, but some questions still remain. Do undercover police officers use these strategies any differently from cooperating witnesses? What makes these conversational strategies so powerful? Why does it take a linguist to identify and analyze these strategies? Can linguistic analysis help distinguish truth from lying and deception? If these conversational strategies are so commonly used in everyday life, why do targets continue to be caught by them? Why is forensic linguistic analysis used mostly by the defense and not by the prosecution? Do the requirements of justice require even higher standards for obtaining clear and unambiguous evidence than exist in most of life's conversational contexts? And finally, what can be done to avoid indictments and convictions growing out of the unfair use of these conversational strategies?

1. Do Cooperating Witnesses and Law Enforcement Officers Use the Same or Different Conversational Strategies in Their Undercover Operations?

To varying degrees, the cooperating witnesses who tape-recorded their conversations with targets appeared to favor the strategies of blocking, ambiguity, not taking "no" for an answer, scripting, lying about what was critical information for the target to know, withholding information, along with an occasional hit and run. As a group, the undercover police appeared to favor using the strategies of blocking, refusing to take "no" for an answer, and various forms of scripting the targets in what to say. The police made more use than cooperating witnesses of the strategies of camouflaging the illegality of the proposed actions and the hit-and-run strategy. Curiously, the police in these cases made only limited use of the ambiguity strategy that was so prominent in the work of cooperating witnesses. On the whole, however, even with this limited sample of twelve undercover cases, there was a strong similarity by both the police and cooperating witnesses in their uses of the eleven conversational strategies.

From the cases described here, it is clear that even though cooperating witnesses and policemen use most of the same strategies, they tend to use different strategies in different contexts. The circumstances of each case seem to have suggested which strategies might work best. For this reason, it seemed prudent to describe a number of different cases concerning a variety of types of crime. For the sake of convenience, the following is a brief summary comparison of such similarities and differences.

The Conversational Strategies of Cooperating Witnesses

In the Cullen Davis case (chapter 4), cooperating witness David McCrory's power came from the uses of ambiguity and manipulating his hidden microphone. From the prosecution's perspective, McCrory succeeded in getting Davis to agree to have his wife and other people murdered. McCrory's ambiguity created the illusion that Davis was asking McCrory to find a hit man when, in fact, Davis was talking about continuing to have McCrory spy on the alleged sexual misbehavior of his wife. McCrory's power of microphone manipulation created the illusion that Davis had agreed to have his wife and others killed when, in fact, Davis was out of normal hearing distance and was simply continuing his ongoing topic about the excuses needed to explain McCrory's absences from work to his boss. McCrory's conversational power of the hit-and-run strategy was also used in this case when, after finally mentioning the "got [him] dead" expression, he quickly exited the car and fled.

In the murder case of Alan Mackerley (chapter 5), cooperating witness Bill Anderson first used the conversational power of the retell strategy, hoping that Mackerley would inculpate himself. After this strategy yielded nothing satisfying, he next tried to get Mackerley to script him in what to tell the police. Another dead end. His final and somewhat desperate use of conversational power was to tell Mackerley an outright lie, which also failed when Mackerley caught him in his deception.

In the purchase of stolen property case of Prakesh Patel and his employee, Daniel Houston (chapter 6), a cooperating witness and an undercover cop worked together, using several powerful conversational strategies. By representing illegality clearly to Houston but vaguely to Patel, they carried out a version of the conversational strategy of withholding important information. They also interrupted and overlapped Patel in critical parts of the conversations, blocking later listeners, such as juries, from learning what Patel was trying to say at those times. The agent camouflaged the illegality of their action by calling it "legitimate" and by advising Patel that his "hands are staying clean." Finally, they used the strategy of refusing to take Patel's "no" for an answer.

The business fraud case of Paul Webster and Joe Marino (chapter 7) was fraught with the powerful strategy of ambiguity. Commonly used everyday words and expressions such as "quietly," "clean it up," "credibility," "profit sharing," "putting it away," "quid pro quo," "crafty," "hiccup," "involved," "exposure," and "beyond the norm" were used to give the illusion that they referred to something illegal.

The contract fraud conspiracy case against David Smith (chapter 8) was also characterized by the cooperating witness's use of the conversational power of ambiguity, accompanied by a lack of specificity in referencing, both of which were pointed out at trial and contributed to Smith's acquittal.

The prosecutor in Paul Manziel's bribery case (chapter 9) was apparently fooled by the shabby undercover work of the relatively unmonitored cooperating witness. The tape recordings did not make clear when

Manziel was actually present and it became apparent that the tapes suspiciously were turned off and electronic static was produced at times when Manziel's defense might have benefited most. The power of the person controlling the tape recording was never more apparent.

In the sexual misconduct case of Dr. Joseph Mussina (chapter 10), a patient used the conversational power strategy of scripting by asking her doctor to give her directives about what to say to her husband and by scripting apologies for what the doctor had allegedly "done to" her. The conversational power of scripting is magnified when utterances have the power to incriminate the targets.

The Conversational Strategies Used by Police Investigators

Part 3 showed that there is relatively little difference between the way cooperating witnesses used these eleven conversational strategies and the way they were used by the police during their interrogations of suspects.

Camouflaged illegality was the major conversational strategy used by the Visa fraud investigator in the obstruction of justice case of Brian Lett (chapter 11). The investigator used expressions that had legal surface meanings but were used by the prosecution to connote illegal acts. Getting nowhere in particular with these, investigator Edwards finally resorted to using the word, "steal." Before Lett could say any more than a disappointed "oh," Edwards used the conversational strategy of the "hit and run" and changed the subject before Lett could respond further.

Camouflage was also the major powerful conversational strategy used by corporate security officer Graham in the purchasing stolen property case against Tariq Shalash (chapter 12). Graham, along with the city policeman who worked with him, made only a minor and confusing effort to represent their goods as stolen property. When the agent eventually used this word, it was camouflaged in a conditional grammatical construction, "you *can* steal" rather than a more explicit, "we stole." Even as he uttered it, however, he camouflaged it by lowering his voice, potentially preventing Shalash from hearing or understanding what he said. Shalash apparently heard enough, however, for he quickly replied that he had never wanted stolen merchandise and told him so, but the agent ignored his functional "no" response and went right on as though it was never said.

The evidence in the Wenatchee sex ring case (chapter 13) included no tape recordings of the detective's interviews with his suspects. Here linguistic analysis had to be based on written records and trial testimony. Even such secondary data can be powerful, however, since it gave many indications that detective Robert Perez used the conversational power of blocking, interrupting and shouting down the people he interviewed. He also refused to accept their claims of innocence and he scripted many of the children and, especially, many uneducated and illiterate adults, about what they should say on record.

In the solicitation to murder case of Mohammed Arshad (chapter 14), the undercover policeman used the conversational strategies of ambiguity, the hit and run, interruption, scripting, and refusing to take "no" for an answer as he exerted his conversational power over Arshad. This practice was particularly offensive in a situation involving cross-cultural issues and a target who was emotionally stressed to the extreme.

The detectives in the Jerry Townsend mass murder case (chapter 15) manipulated the tape recorder in a regrettable display of how not to use the conversational power assigned to them by their superordinate status. They interrupted Townsend at critical moments, inaccurately restated what he said, and scripted him in what he should say, especially during the many periods when the tape recorder was turned off.

2. What Makes These Conversational Strategies So Powerful in Undercover Law Enforcement Operations?

To my knowledge, the extent of the conversational power of these eleven strategies has not been fully explored in the research literature to date. Much has been said about the power assigned to the person asking questions and considerable attention has been given to how ambiguity works, and how, when, and why interruption and overlap occur in some contexts. Even more has been said about powerless language features, but not about how the strategies discussed here operate. The undercover legal context seemed to be a fertile place to find and identify these strategies. Logic and experience would tell us that these eleven strategies were not invented by undercover law enforcement, and it is not difficult to think of everyday conversations in which they can occur. If they are as commonly used to exert power as I suspect that they are, one should not be surprised that they are even more powerful in undercover tape situations. I believe that there are three reasons for this.

1. Some of Them Are So Commonplace and Familiar That They Are Not Very Noticeable to Targets

The ambiguity strategy appears to be the most common in the cases described in this book, perhaps because most people are so accustomed to its occurrence in everyday, nonplanned discourse. Ambiguity is a relatively unmarked form of the use of conversational power, since we encounter ambiguity all the time and we may not be ready for, or alert to, its more deliberate uses. The same might be said for interruptions and overlaps, which also commonly occur often in naturally occurring conversation. Our very familiarity with hearing ambiguous expressions and being interrupted or overlapped are likely to make them more difficult to detect as powerful conversation strategies intended to deceive. In undercover tapes or, for that matter, in police interrogations, or even in verbal exchanges at trial, they can be very dangerous unless these power moves are recognized, clarified, and corrected.

2. Some of Them, though Noticeable, Even Irritating, Do Not Arouse a Particular Suspicion

We are somewhat less accustomed to the conversational power of deception that is created deliberately by others when we are asked to retell something that has happened in the past, when someone tries to script us in what to say, when someone introduces something questionable then hits and runs by changing the subject quickly to a very different topic, and when our conversations are contaminated by the insertion of foul language, tough talk, ethnic jokes, or references to irrelevant criminal or otherwise untoward acts. Although these things may be common in everyday talk, they can rankle and become offensive on at least some occasions. Seldom, however, do we think of them as efforts to give the illusion that we are being set up to appear to be saying or doing something illegal. For this reason, they too present grave dangers to targets or suspects unless lawyers, judges, law enforcement officers, and, especially, juries are taught to recognize them for what they are.

3. Some of Them Are So Deceptive That We Don't Even Know What Hit Us

Most deceptive of all are the conversation strategies of camouflaging illegality, lying about important things that we need to know, and refusing to take our "no" for an answer. Camouflaging something illegal as legal is, in itself, a form of lying, which, if not recognized, can easily lead a target into serious trouble with the law. It can be argued that lying is essential in some aspects of covert operations, but there is a vast difference between the sort of scenario-lying necessary and proper in undercover work, and lying about critical facts upon which the targets have to rely to make decisions either to commit illegal acts or to reject them. All such uses of these powerful conversation strategies should be exposed for what they are.

The conversational strategy of deliberately withholding important information that a target needs to know in order to make an informed decision about whether or not to commit a crime is particularly offensive when used by law enforcement officers or by the cooperating witnesses under their supervision. The same is true for the act of purposely isolating targets in ways that prevent them from acquiring such information. Targets have no way of knowing what is happening to them in such circumstances and are powerless to repair anything. The resulting tape recordings, however, may make it appear that they knew, a sad power move for law enforcement to be proud of. Again, careful linguistic analysis of the conversations should point this out.

3. Why Does It Take a Linguist to Point Out These Things?

Once they are exposed, the conversational strategies used by undercover law enforcement agents and cooperating witnesses described here may seem pretty obvious. Language is like that. We don't notice things until they're called to our attention. It's a bit ironic that linguists often call attention to little things that others don't notice but, once these little things are pointed out, they seem so obvious that one wonders why a linguist was needed in the first place. So, once these conversational strategies are described, as I have here, they may not seem all that new or surprising. We've all been in situations where someone has blocked our conversation by interrupting or overlapping what we were trying to say. We probably marked it as annoying but we usually don't think it necessary to give great importance to the outcome. The interrupter may have seemed rude, but few if any long-term consequences are likely to result. Discourse analysts are experts in discovering the conversational significance of such things as interruption, overlapping, and other forms of blocking.

Likewise, we've all been in situations when other persons have used ambiguous language to us and we didn't quite get the meaning. Of course we always have the option of stopping the speakers right then and there to ask what in the world they meant. But this could seem impolite and could cost us something in our social relationship with those persons. So our most common response is to wait it out, hoping that the meaning might become clear as the conversation progresses. Linguists are trained in semantics and are experts in analyzing language ambiguities and their consequences.

We also have become accustomed to situations in which other persons refuse to take our "no" for an answer. Sales encounters easily come to mind, as do reports of young women who try to ward off the romantic advances of young men. Nothing new here either. It's part of everyday experience. Since not all "no" responses are explicit and direct, linguists trained in pragmatics are skilled at helping to discover and analyze them.

It's quite possible that we have personally experienced the hit-and-run strategy, although we probably didn't recognize it while it was actually happening to us. The speaker who drops a verbal bomb into the conversation, then quickly changes the subject to something very different, is perhaps unknowingly relying on the recency principle—people tend to respond to the most recent topic on the table and they tend to ignore the topics brought up just before it. If the dropped topic is a crucial one that the speaker really doesn't want us to comment on, this strategy works well for that speaker. In most of life, there are no serious consequences other than that the initiator of this topic can say later that he didn't hear us make any objection to it. Of course we didn't object to it; we followed the speaker's lead to the newly changed topic. So there's nothing really new or different here either. There are linguists who are experts in such things as the use of the recency principle and other forms of conversational behavior to help point this out.

When a person inaccurately restates something that we said earlier, we need to be on our toes to catch the inaccuracy. Sometimes we are careful enough to catch it, but at other times we may be so occupied with the direction of our own thoughts that we simply let it pass unnoticed. It happens all the time. Even though it would seem that the average listener could catch such inconsistencies, they often don't—not even lawyers, judges, law enforcement officers, or jurors who have the advantage of playing the tape over and over again. Linguists are trained to attend to minute details of conversation and to note consistencies and inconsistencies as they occur.

All of our lives, beginning at our mother's knee, people have been scripting us about what we should say, so when this occurs it is not all that new or surprising. This sometimes comes under the category of advice: "Why don't you tell him to get lost?" "If I were you, I'd tell her to get a new boyfriend," "Say to him, 'I'm the best man for the job.'" When people repeat words or sentences that have been scripted for them, they are a step away from giving their own personal statements. Again, discourse analysts can help identify this practice and attest to its consequences.

In contrast, we often aren't fully aware of it when another person camouflages the information they give to us. If there are reasons to suspect the motives of the speaker, our ears may perk up, as when our teenage son tells us that all of his friends are really safe drivers. We may also be totally unaware of occasions when important information that we need to know is being withheld from us. If we have no particular reason to suspect anything, we tend to dismiss camouflage as truth, and we have no reason to know that any information has been withheld from us, much less that it might be important. In undercover operations and interrogations such as those described in this book, camouflaging and withholding information can be crucially important. Linguists are trained to identify such conversational strategies and describe their overall significance to a given conversation.

4. Can Linguistic Analysis Identify Lying and Deception?

There are some things that linguistic analysis can do to help identify lying and deception. For example, a man who claims to be born and bred in Akron, Ohio, but does not recognize the term, "devil strip" to describe the grassy area between the sidewalk and the curb, may not be telling the truth about his origin. There are other regional and social identifiers of this type, including clues to a person's gender, race, ethnicity, occupation, religious background, age, and education. But they are just that—clues. As such, they fall into the category of "investigative" insights rather than absolute identifiers that can stand up under rigorous cross-examination in court. One problem is that people are highly mobile these days and they tend to pick up language patterns from the places where they live, the people they admire, and the jargon of their workplace. I have found that the most effective contribution that a linguist can make to the question of whether or not a person is lying is to search the text for inconsistencies in discourse patterns (Shuy 1998; Galasinski 2000).

A cooperating witness or detective who lies to a target or suspect poses a different problem. Should targets be able to tell when they are being lied to? As research has shown, people are not very good lie detectors (Miller and Stiff 1993; Robinson 1996). Ekman and O'Sullivan's research on several occupational groups, including police investigators, judges, psychiatrists, and federal polygraph experts, showed that representatives of these occupations were not significantly more accurate at detecting lying than were average college students (1991). On the whole, humans are only slightly more accurate about distinguishing truth from deception than a flip of the coin might tell them. And targets in criminal investigations are no better at detecting deception than anyone else. From the undercover operative's perspective, lying and deception pose a moral dilemma that should be addressed. Ekman (1985) explains that there are two ways to lie (he equates lying with deceiving): to conceal and to falsify. The person who conceals is withholding information without saying anything untrue, but it is still deceptive. A person who falsifies takes the additional step of intentionally presenting false information as if it were true. Bok (1989, p. 13) defines a lie as "any intentionally deceptive message." Coleman and Kaye (1981) hypothesize that lying has three features: a false statement, the intent to deceive, and knowledge of the falseness of what is reported. Intentionality appears to be the crucial characteristic of deception and lying, and a person's intentions are very difficult, if not impossible, to assess.

It is not within my province to determine whether undercover cooperating witnesses and police investigators are always being intentionally deceptive or whether they are using these conversational strategies more accidentally, perhaps even calling on their lifelong skill in doing this in everyday speech. With the exceptions of the obviously intentional strategies of camouflaging illegality, giving blatantly false information to targets, and withholding crucial information about what is important and what is not, it really makes little difference whether the other conversational strategies described in this book are used intentionally or not (although I continue to suspect that they were used intentionally). Whether deceptive or not, the language used is the language used. It is the evidence in a criminal case and, as such, it is susceptible to linguistic analysis.

The linguist (or anyone else for that matter) cannot get into the minds of the speakers and listeners to determine exactly what they intended and what they understood. But the language used is evidence of the range of possibilities that could be intended by the speakers and could be comprehended by the listeners. When such language is ambiguous, blocked, overlapped, scripted, interrupted, camouflaged, hit and run, and the "no" response is ignored, defense attorneys, prosecutors, judges, law enforcement officers, and juries should be taught to recognize that the targets are forced to guess, infer, tolerate unclarity, and hope that they can ultimately figure out what was meant. Even worse yet, these same attorneys, prosecutors, judges, law enforcement officers, and juries are forced to do the very same thing when they listen to tapes containing these conversational strategies—to guess and infer the meaning of what was said and understood on the tapes.

5. Why Do Targets Get Trapped by These Commonplace Conversational Strategies?

If these conversational strategies are so common, why do targets continue to get caught by them? To begin with, just like everyone else, they are unaware of what is happening to them. Conversation has certain principles that are absolutely necessary if effective communication is to happen at all. One of the most quoted scholars on these principles is the philosopher, H. P. Grice, who first codified the rules by which conversation could be constructed when information exchange is its only goal (1967). Simply put, Grice's four maxims are:

1. Say as much as necessary and no more
2. Tell the truth
3. Be relevant to the topic
4. Be clear and unambiguous

Listeners draw implicatures (context-dependent meanings) when speakers flout these maxims. When speakers say something that is seemingly irrelevant, unclear, too much, or too little, listeners tend to try to make sense of it rather than risk asking potentially impolite questions such as, "What on earth do you mean by that?" or "Why are you telling me all this anyway?" In conversation we have only a limited number of such chits to redeem, lest the speaker think of us as impolite, or stupid, or worse. The convention of politeness tends to discourage such requests for clarification and outright objections (Brown and Levinson 1987). Speakers expect their conversational partners to refrain from imposing, to give options, and to be friendly (Lakoff 1979).

These expectations frame a perfect situation for undercover operations to work effectively for law enforcement in its attempt to capture language crimes. Unfortunately, these expectations also work well to help them create the illusion of crime where it does not exist. Like the rest of us, unsuspecting targets tend to act as though these maxims are being followed, and they are, like the rest of us, reluctant to flag seeming violations of them, mostly out of conventional conversational rules of behavior. Targets, like the rest of us, are also bound to the conventional rules of politeness. So when a speaker tells an ethnically offensive joke, it is difficult even for offended listeners to object very strongly. Instead, many people smile politely, despite the fact that they may be morally disgusted or even offended. They may also be offended when the other speaker begins to use foul language, but they are often too polite to call this to the speaker's attention. They may believe that the other person is off-topic or irrelevant, but because of a sense of politeness, they may not be able to bring themselves to comment on the other person's conversational offense. If an ambiguous hint statement is offered by a speaker, a listener may often simply interpret it in the most benign fashion. Thus the expectations of fairness, truthfulness, relevance, and clarity override the targets' possible objections, setting them up for the illusion of having agreed to the other person's suggestions. Some undercover tape operations, in particular, take advantage of these things.

6. Why Doesn't the Prosecution Use Forensic Linguistic Analysis of This Type?

It should be rather clear that the focus of this book is about the unfairness of some of the conversational strategies used by law enforcement in its effort to capture criminals. As such, it may appear that I am biased in favor of the defense and against the prosecution. Nothing could be more wrong. The simple truth is that law enforcement seldom calls on forensic linguists to assist them with their cases. Here, my own experience in helping to pioneer the application of linguistics to the area of law in criminal cases over the past twenty-five years is relevant. On the few occasions when prosecutors have called on me for help, they have put restrictions on my participation that call into question their real motives for asking for my assistance. In any of the cases discussed above, if the prosecution had asked for my help, I would have advised them of the problems that their cases presented, especially when the undercover operative used the conversational strategies that were described and discussed. Better yet, the best advice I could give would occur before indictments were even brought. Good intelligence analysis does not depend on questionable, even debatable, tape-recorded data.

It appears that law enforcement officers and prosecutors don't often want the help of forensic linguists in such cases. They have tape recordings as evidence that can be deceptively convincing to juries. I often advise defense attorneys that they begin their cases with two strikes against them: the indictment and the tapes. From there it can be an uphill battle to convince jurors that the indictment was misguided and that the mere existence of tapes does not prove the government's case.

Of the some five hundred criminal cases in which I have either testified or consulted over the past twenty-five years, I have been called on officially by the government only eleven times. Meanwhile, virtually every time I have testified for the defense at trial, the prosecutor has made it a point to ask me whether or not I had ever testified on behalf of the prosecution in a criminal case. The point of this question, of course, was to try to show the jury that I was just a hired gun for the defense. In response, if given the chance to give more than a "yes" or "no" answer, I could say that I had consulted with the prosecution in two extortion cases in New Hampshire between 1987 and 1989, in two obstruction of justice cases involving federal Judge Aguilar of San Francisco and federal Judge Nixon of Mississippi in 1990, in a police misconduct and narcotics case in the District of Columbia in 1994, in the use of illegal campaign funds by a U.S. Congressperson in 1994, in the FBI's Unabomber investigation in 1996, in the FBI's Arizona train sabotage case in 1996, in the Canadian Royal Mounted Police Loki bomber case on Prince Edward Island in 1997, in the FBI's Atlanta Olympic bombing case in 1997, and in the FBI's Gary, Indiana, bomb threat case in 1997. However, even though I *consulted* on these eleven cases, in not one of them did the prosecutors ask me to testify.

I could also respond that I had testified for the prosecution for the U.S. House of Representatives and the U.S. Senate in the successful impeachment of Federal Judge Alcee Hastings of Florida, but this did not qualify as a criminal trial, at least not in the minds of prosecutors who questioned me on the witness stand in other cases. Nor did my testimony before the U.S. House of Representatives in the massive oversight investigation of the FBI, carried out in 1982 by the U.S. House of Representative's Committee on the Judiciary, count in the minds of the prosecution. Neither of these seemed to satisfy the prosecutors as evidence of my working for the government instead of against it.

But let's go back to the eleven criminal cases in which I carried out my analyses and was not asked to present them in court. After the U.S. District Attorney in the two New Hampshire cases and the cases of the two federal judges left the government to become a defense attorney, he revealed to me that he hadn't wanted me to testify because such action would have legitimized my testimony in the courtroom. If I were to testify for the prosecution, even one time, other prosecutors would no longer be able to celebrate that I testified only for the defense. From this they could gain an advantage by making me look like the defense's hired gun. Later, interestingly enough, this same attorney, now working for defendants, has called on me to assist him several times with his cases.

A different reason for not wanting me to testify was given by the U.S. District Attorney who called on me to analyze the tape recordings in the Washington, D.C., police misconduct/narcotics case. He told me point-blank from the outset that he wanted my analysis as rebuttal testimony just in case the defendants happened to use a forensic linguist themselves. They didn't, and so once again I didn't get to testify for the prosecution. The same was true in the campaign funds abuse case, where the U.S. District Attorney made it equally clear that she only wanted my analysis as a fail safe against the possibility of the defendant calling on a linguist for help. Both of these cases took place in the District of Columbia, where I lived and was well known in both the defense and prosecution communities, making me suspect that the attorneys were simply co-opting me and trying to make sure that I didn't testify for the defense.

The Unabomber case had a different wrinkle. In 1995 I was called by FBI agents first to examine the written messages that accompanied the bombs sent to various people over a period of seventeen years. Shortly thereafter, the Unabomber's famous "Manifesto" was published simultaneously by *The Washington Post* and *The New York Times*, providing an additional wealth of information that might give clues to who this man really was.

Earlier, the FBI had opined in its psychological profile that the Unabomber was a young man, relatively uneducated, living on either the East or West coasts and probably working at some sort of menial job. I explained that I could provide a linguistic profile (as opposed to their psychological profile) based only on the clues offered in the Unabomber's written materials. My completed report showed among other things that the Unabomber's use of language gave strong evidence that he was middle-aged rather than young, that his geographical background was the Chicago area, that he was highly educated (my report said that if he had a PhD, it was not in the humanities or social sciences), that he had probably spent some time in northern California, and that he was Catholic. All of these turned out to be accurate. I make absolutely no claim that my analysis led to the capture of Theodore Kaczynski. As it is now well known, his own brother recognized the similarities of what was written in the Manifesto from correspondence that Ted Kaczynski had with him in the past, eventually leading to his capture in a forest near Lincoln, Montana. All the same, it's hard for me to imagine that I was not working for the government in this case.

In the Arizona train sabotage case, a very brief and cryptic handwritten note found at the wreck scene provided few linguistic clues with which to identify the writer. The best that I could offer was that the author was not likely to be one of their extant suspects, since their regional dialect features were inconsistent with the language used in the note left at the scene.

In the Gary bomb-threat case, my report helped investigators obtain an admission of guilt from the threat writer. They showed him my linguistic comparison of the threat letters with samples of the suspect's known writings and he quickly admitted to the crime. The match was very close in terms of syntax, lexicon, and mechanics.

So why do I say that it is difficult to work for the prosecution? For one thing, my experience shows that law enforcement and the prosecution seem to be more interested in winning a case than in discovering the truth. I suppose this should not be surprising in an adversarial legal system such as ours since defense attorneys are no less immune to this. But it has been disappointing to not be asked by the prosecution to help them with their cases and to testify on their behalf simply because such testimony might legitimize the objectivity and standing of forensic linguistics in the courts. It is equally disappointing to be co-opted by the prosecution simply to be prevented from working for the defense. Good linguistic analysis can reveal such things as the powerful conversational strategies described in this book, but linguists are seldom called by the prosecution to do so.

7. Why Is the Use of These Conversational Strategies More Significant in Police Undercover Operations Than It Is in Everyday Life?

The major difference between the everyday use of these conversational strategies and their use in undercover operations is that the search for justice demands that evidence contain a higher degree of clarity that isn't always as necessary in the rest of our daily existence. In many of life's situations, we can guess, infer, or wait for clarity to happen. But when the prosecution puts tape recordings of such evidence before a jury, these everyday response strategies can be dangerously damaging. When targets are confused by such strategies in a criminal investigation, it is difficult for a jury to walk in their shoes and to see what was actually going on at the time it was happening. This also puts juries in the same awkward situation that the targets found themselves in when their conversations were tape-recorded. Juries now have to do the same sort of guessing and inferring that the targets had to do. Juries should not be expected to have to guess or infer when they make their decisions. Prosecutors should not have to let them do this. Defense attorneys should prevent this from happening.

8. What Can Be Done about the Unfair Use of These Conversational Strategies?

Inequality of power is a common problem of human life. Sometimes such inequality can be dealt with amiably through well-meaning negotiation, before angry responses or even litigation have to take place. The fact that the inequalities created by powerful conversational strategies described in this book don't always reach the level of consciousness makes their remedy all the more difficult. Like walking or riding a bicycle, most people have learned how to speak their native language so well that they don't really know what they are doing as they speak it. It takes careful descriptions of what is actually going on to bring this to light. This, of course, is one of the important goals of linguistic analysis.

For this reason, it seemed necessary to call attention to the eleven common yet powerful conversational strategies described in this book. Forensic linguists can be alerted to the way language is used in undercover cases and to look for these strategies as they analyze tape cases. Other primary audiences, are the defense attorneys, prosecutors, and law enforcement officers who plan and carry out undercover operations by tape-recording conversations of targets. It's always better to avoid a problem before it happens.

Defense attorneys who have clients who appear to be innocent of some or all of the criminal counts for which they are charged may find these descriptions helpful in dealing with the tape-recorded conversations in which some or all of these strategies were employed. Even though attorneys are often very skilled in how to use language, they may not be skilled enough to carry out analyses of the type described in this book. It would behoove them to look more carefully and deeply into how law enforcement representatives use language with their clients, especially in undercover tape cases. Alternatively, it could prove to be prudent for them to call on linguists to help them with this task.

It is hoped that prosecutors will be alerted to the way these strategies were used as they decide whether or not to indict suspects, based on such language evidence. Again, however, even the considerable language skills of prosecutors may not enable them to recognize the subtle ways that undercover operatives, consciously or unconsciously, can and do use these conversational strategies unfairly to paint their targets into a corner. And if defense attorneys call on linguists to point these things out, prosecutors would be wise to do the same. The big difference here is that prosecutors get the first chance to do so, before indictments are brought and before the time and expense of a trial takes place. Such action would surely be economical for the court system, to say nothing of furthering the cause of justice.

Finally, law enforcement officers who supervise and monitor cooperating witnesses who tape-record their targets or who themselves undertake such undercover operations may find this information about powerful conversational strategies helpful. They can be trained to develop an active and conscious awareness about how these strategies can be recognized and used by defense attorneys on behalf of their clients before the tapes become evidence at trial. Such awareness can prepare them for what might be an uncomfortable cross-examination. They can also use such knowledge to decide whether or not to continue or abandon their undercover operations. I am aware of no manuals of undercover tape operations or training programs that deal with these strategies at present. It is not difficult to imagine how law enforcement officers can be taught how to engage in conversations that actually capture a language crime rather than merely creating the illusion that a crime has happened when their own taped evidence does not show that it has.

Criminals should be caught and punished, but only by using fair and just methods, not by the unfair uses of ambiguity, not by blocking what targets might have to say, not by hitting and running, not by contaminating the tape with irrelevant information, not by isolating targets from information necessary for them to decide the next steps to take, not by ignoring the targets' attempts to say "no" to the enterprise, not by inaccurately restating what the targets said, not by withholding information that targets need in order to make decisions, not by lying about important information that affects the targets' decision making, and not by scripting targets in what to say on the tapes. The system of justice could hope for a lot better.

REFERENCES CITED

Ainsworth-Vaughn, Nancy. 1998. *Claiming Power in Doctor-Patient Talk.* New York: Oxford University Press.
Bateson, Gregory. 1972. *Towards an Ecology of Mind.* New York: Chandler. 1972.
Bok, Sissela. *Lying.* 1989. New York: Vintage.
Bolinger, Dwight. 1980. *Language: The Loaded Weapon.* London: Longman.
Brown, Penelope, and Stephen Levinson. 1987. *Politeness: Some Universals in Language Use.* Cambridge: Cambridge University Press, 1978.
Burbules, Nicholas. "A theory of power in education." *Educational Theory* 36 (Spring 1986): 95–114.
Cameron, Deborah et al. 1999. "Power/knowledge: the politics of social science." In *The Discourse Reader,* edited by Adam Jaworski and Nikolas Coupland, 141–57. London: Routledge.
Ceci, Stephen J., and Maggie Bruck. 1995. *Jeopardy in the Courtroom.* Washington, D.C.: American Psychological Association.
Coleman, Linda, and Paul Kay. 1981. "Prototype semantics: the English verb 'lie.'" *Language* 57, no. 1 (1986): 26–44.
Conley, John M., and William M. O'Barr. 1998. *Just Words: Law, Language, and Power.* Chicago: University of Chicago Press.
Cotterill, Janet. *Language and Power in Court.* 2003. Houndmills, Basingstoke, Hampshire: Palgrave Macmillan.
Craig, Robert T., and Karen Tracy. 1983. *Conversational Coherence.* Beverly Hills, CA: Sage.
de Klerk, Vivian. "Language and the law: who has the upper hand?" In *Africa and Applied Linguistics,* ed. Sinfree Makoni, 89–103. AILA Review 2003, vol. 16.
Ekman, Paul. 1985. *Telling Lies.* New York: Norton.
Ekman, Paul, and Maurine O'Sullivan. 1991. "Who can catch a liar?" *American Psychologist,* 46, 913–20.

U.S. House. *FBI Undercover Operations: Report of the Subcommittee on Civil and Constitutional Rights of the Committee on the Judiciary, House of Representatives Together with Dissenting Views.* 1984. Washington, D.C.: U.S. Government Printing Office.
Foucault, M. 1997. *Power/Knowledge.* Hemel Hempsted: Harvester.
Fraser, Bruce. 1999. "What Are Discourse Markers?" *Journal of Pragmatics* 31, 931-52.
Galasinski, Dariusz. 2000. *The Language of Deception.* Thousand Oaks, Calif.: Sage Publications.
Goffman, Erving. 1967. *Interaction Ritual.* Garden City, N.Y.: Anchor.
———. 1974. *Frame Analysis.* New York: Harper & Row.
———. 1979. "Footing." *Semiotica* 25, vol. 1, nos. 1/2: (1979): 1–29.
Goodwin, Charles. "Professional vision." *American Anthropologist* 96, no. 3 (1996): 606–33.
Grice, H. P. 1967. "Logic and conversation." William James Lectures, Harvard University, Cambridge, Mass. Reprinted in *Syntax and Semantics.* Vol. 3, *Speech Acts*, edited by Peter Cole and Jerry Morgan, 43–58. New York: Cambridge University Press, 1975.
Gumperz, John. 1982. *Discourse Strategies.* Cambridge: Cambridge University Press.
Hansell, Mark, and Cheryl S. Ajirotutu. 1982. "Negotiating interpretations in interethnic settings." In *Language and Social Identity*, ed. John Gumperz, 85–94. Cambridge: Cambridge University Press.
Harris, Sandra. "Questions as a mode of control in magistrates' courts." *International Journal of the Sociology of Language* 49 (1984): 5–28.
———. 1994. "Ideological exchanges in British magistrates courts." In *Language and the Law*, ed. John Gibbons, 156–70. London: Longman.
Heritage, J. Maxwell. 1984. "A change-of-state token and aspects of its sequential placement." In *Structures of Social Action: Studies in Conversation Analysis*, edited by J. M. Atkinson and J. Heritage, 299–345. Cambridge: Cambridge University Press.
Honneth, Axel. 1991. *The Critique of Power: Reflective Stages in a Critical Social Theory.* Cambridge Mass.: MIT Press.
Inbau, Fred E., John E. Reid, and Joseph P. Buckley. 1986. *Criminal Interrogation and Confessions.* Baltimore: Williams and Wilkins.
Kelly, John F., and Phillip K. Wearne. 1998. *Tainting Evidence.* New York: Free Press.
Labov, William. 2003. "Uncovering the event structure in narrative." *Linguistics, Language, and the Real World: Discourse and Beyond*, edited by Deborah Tannen and James E. Alatis, 63–83. Washington, D.C.: Georgetown University Press.
Lakoff, Robin. "Language in women's place." *Language in Society* 2 (1973): 45–80.
———. 1979. "Stylistic strategies within a grammar of style." In *Annals of the New York Academy of Science*, edited by Judith Orasanu, Miriam Slater, and Lenore Adler 327, 553–578
———. 1989. *Talking Power.* 1989. New York: Basic.
———. *The Language War.* 2000. Berkeley and Los Angeles: University of California Press.
Leo, Richard, and R. Ofshe. "The consequences of false confession, deprivation of liberty and miscarriages of justice in the age of psychological interrogation." *Journal of Criminal Law and Criminology* 88, no. 2, (1997):429–96.

McCullough, David. 2001. *John Adams.* New York: Simon & Schuster.
Miller, Gerald R., and James B. Stiff. 1993. *Deceptive Communication.* Newbury Park Calif.: Sage Publications.
Ng, Hung Sik, and James J. Bradac. 1993. *Power in Language.* Newbury Park Calif.: Sage Publications.
O'Barr, William M. 1982. *Linguistic Evidence: Language, Power, and Strategy in the Courtroom.* New York: Academic Press.
Ofshe, Richard, and Richard Leo. "The decision to confess falsely." *Denver Law Review,* 74, 4 (1997): 913–1122.
Philips, Susan U. "The social organization of questions and answers in courtroom discourse." *Text* 4, no. 1–3 (1985): 228–48.
Poole, Debra A., and Michael E. Lamb. 1998. *Investigative Interviews of Children.* Washington, D.C.: American Psychological Association.
Robinson, W. Peter. 1996. *Deceit, Delusion, and Detection.* Thousand Oaks, CA: Sage.
Sandoval, Vincent A. 2003. "Strategies to avoid interview contamination." *Law Enforcement Bulletin* 72, no. 10 (2003): 1–12.
Scheck, Barry, Peter Neufeld, and Jim Dwyer. 2000. *Actual Innocence.* New York: Doubleday.
Schiffrin, Deborah. 1987. *Discourse Markers.* Cambridge: Cambridge University Press.
———. "Speaking for another." 1993. In *Framing Discourse,* ed. Deborah Tannen, 231–63. New York: Oxford University Press.
Shuy, Roger W. 1993. *Language Crimes.* Oxford: Blackwell.
———. 1998. *The Language of Confession, Interrogation and Deception.* Thousand Oaks, Calif: Sage Publications.
———. 2001. "Using a linguist in money laundering trials." In *White Collar Crime,* F19–F38. Chicago: American Bar Association.
Solan, Lawrence M. 1993. *The Language of Judges.* Chicago: University of Chicago Press.
Sornig, Karl. 1989. "Some remarks on linguistic strategies of persuasion." In *Language Power and Ideology,* edited by Ruth Wodak, 95–114. Amsterdam: John Benjamins.
Stygall, Gail. 1994. *Trial Language: Differential Discourse Processing and Discursive Formation.* Amsterdam: John Benjamins.
Tannen, Deborah. 1987. "Remarks on discourse and power." In *Power through Discourse,* ed. Leah Kedar, 3–10. Norwood, N.J.: Ablex.
———. 1993. *Framing in Discourse.* New York: Oxford University Press.
———. *Gender and Discourse.* 1994. New York: Oxford University Press.
———. 2003. "Power Maneuvers or Connection Maneuvers? Ventriloquizing in Family Interaction." In *Linguistics, Language, and the Real World: Discourse and Beyond,* edited by Deborah Tannen and James E. Alatis, 50–62. Washington, D.C.: Georgetown University Press.
———. 2004. "Talking the Dog." Research on Language and Social Interaction 37:4
Tiersma, Peter. 1999. *Legal Language.* Chicago: University of Chicago Press.
Van Dijk, Teun, ed. 1985. *Handbook of Discourse Analysis.* Vol. 1. London: Academic Press.

Cases Cited

State of Texas v. Thomas Cullen Davis
No. 16836, Tarrant County, Northern District, Texas
Fort Worth, Texas
State of Florida v. Alan Mackerley
No. 4098-0856, Florida Circuit Court, 6th Judicial District, 2002
Clearwater, Florida
United States v. Prakesh Patel and Daniel Houston
CR-02-152
U.S. District Court for the Western Judicial District of Oklahoma
Oklahoma City, Oklahoma
United States v. Paul Webster and Joe Martino (anonymous at request of counsel)
United States v. David Smith
No. 1: 1997cr00022
U.S. District Court for the Eastern District of Virginia 1997
Alexandria, Virginia
United States v. Paul Manziel
Cause No. 114-0751-03
114th Judicial District Court of Smith County, Texas
Tyler, Texas
State of Idaho v. Joseph Mussina (anonymous by request of counsel)
United States v. Brian Lett
Crim. No. 01-67(1)ADM/AJB
U.S. District Court for the District of Minnesota
Minneapolis, Minnesota
United States v. Tariq Shalash
No. 5:2001cr00093
Eastern District of Kentucky 2001
Lexington, Kentucky
State of Washington v. Doris Green
No. 94-1-00434-5
Superior Court of the State of Washington, Chelan County
Court of Appeals No. 17920-6-111
Wenatchee, Washington
The Crown v. Mohammed Arshad
Her Majesty's High Court
Aberdeen, Scotland
State of Florida v. Jerry Townsend
79-1468, 79-15569
U.S. District Court for Fort Lauderdale, 17th Judicial District, Fort Lauderdale, Florida

INDEX

Adams, Abagail, 17
agenda, 14, 22, 32, 36, 140–141, 182
agreement, 44
Ainsworth-Vaugh, Nancy, 33
aligning, 20
alternative understandings, 15
ambiguity, conversational strategy of, 6, 8–9, 10, 15–16, 34–35, 37, 38, 43, 54, 69–80, 111, 121, 124, 126, 132, 140–41, 144, 146, 148–49, 150–52, 157, 168, 169, 171, 172, 174
apologies, 103
arranged marriages in Muslim culture, 137–38
Arshad, Mohammed. 137–57, 171

bait and switch, 24
Bateson, Gegory, 35
blocking, conversational strategy of. See also creating static, interrupting and overlapping, speaking on behalf of, and manipulating the conversation, 16–17, 34, 60, 63–64, 96, 132, 134, 156, 164, 167, 169, 171, 174
Bok, Sissila, 176
Bollinger, Dwight, 38
Brown, Penelope and Stephen Levinson, 18, 178
Burbules, Nicholas, 32

Cameron, Deborah, 36
camouflaging, conversational strategy of, xi, 24, 34, 37, 60, 64–65, 110, 113, 116, 120–27, 132, 168, 169, 170, 173, 175, 177
Ceci, Stephen J. and Maggie Bruck, 29
changing the subject. See also hit and run 6, 34
Clayton, Representative Billy Clayton, 28
coaching, 21, 29, 53, 83
Cochrane, Johnny, viii
Coleman, Linda and Paul Kay, 176
conditionals, 126, 145, 170
conflict talk, 145
Conley, John and William O'Barr, 36
contamination, conversational strategy of. 22–24, 25, 27, 34, 37, 79, 89–98, 172
context, 16, 46, 48, 104, 123, 125, 144, 168
contextualization clues, 15
conversational strategies, 9, 11, 12, 13–15
coerced confession, 130, 159–64
cooperating witnesses, 10–11, 15, 16, 20, 22, 23, 25, 27, 48, 59, 60–61, 69, 80, 89, 90, 96, 98, 167, 168, 169, 173, 184
cooperative principle, 13

Cotterill, Janet, 38
courtroom language, 36
Craig, Robert and Karen Tracy, 13
creating static on tape, 17

Davis, T. Cullen. 41-49, 118
deception, 4, 24, 28, 127, 172, 173
definite article, 161
deKlerk, Vivian, 36
DeLorean, John Z. 3, 16
directives, 142-57
discourse markers, 48, 97, 115
Driscoll, Amy and Manny Garcia, 163
dummy noun, 62
dummy verb, 15, 43-44, 61-62

Ekman, Paul and Maurine O'Sullivan, 176
electronic recording, 3-4
event structure, underlying, 16
evidence of speaker's presence, 92-93

false confessions, 4
FBI Guidelines, 8-9, 140
"fishing" technique, 83, 113
Foreign Military Financing Program (FMF), 81-88
Forrester, Hugo, 25
Foucalt, M, 31
four step undercover procedure, 7-9
frame of reference, 34, 140-43, 148
framing devices, 35
Frank, Larra and John Hanchette, ix
Fraser, Bruce, 115

Galasinski, Dariuz, 176
Goffman, Erving, 18, 35
Goldstein, Gerald, 91
Goodwin, Charles, viii, ix
grammatical referencing, 105, 145, 146, 150
Green, Doris, 129, 132
greeting and closing routines, 25
Grice, H.P., 13, 178
Gumperz, John, 13

Hansell, Mark and Cheryl S. Ajirotutu, 13

Harris, Sandra, 36
Hatfield, Senator Mark O., 23
Haynes, Richard "Racehorse," 43, 45
Heritage, J. Maxwell, 115
Heymann, Philip, 140
hinting, law enforcement undercover step of, 8, 21, 35, 69-80, 83, 85-86, 87, 111, 113, 144
hit and run, conversational strategy of, 21-22, 37, 49, 79, 94, 115, 152-53, 157, 168, 170, 171, 172, 174, 179
Honneth, Axel, 32
Houston, Daniel, 59-68, 169

ignoring the targets when they say "no," conversational strategy of, 26, 34, 37, 60, 65-68, 127, 132, 134, 139, 153-55, 157, 168-72, 174, 176
implicatures, 178
inaccurate restatement, conversational strategy of, 26-27, 34, 37, 132, 164, 175
Inbau, Fred E., Joseph P. Buckley and John E. Reid, 27
indexicals, 19
inference, 27, 77-78, 80, 112-13, 182
intelligence, gathering and analysis, 10, 11, 16, 29, 88, 179
interrupting and overlapping, conversational strategy of. See also blocking. 6, 9, 17, 19, 38, 40, 45-46, 47-48, 54, 63-64, 111, 115, 134, 151-53, 155, 157, 162, 164, 168, 171, 172, 174
intonation, 44, 145
isolating targets from important information, conversational strategy of, 24-25, 48, 173

Jones, Stephen, 60

Kelly, Congressman Richard, 26, 68
Kelly, John F. and Phillip K. Wearne, x
keys to interpret frames, 35
Krovatin, Gerald, 53

Labov, William, 16
Lakoff, Robin, 31, 33, 36, 38, 178

language bullying, 35
language crimes, definition of, 6
leading questions, 38
legal system, adversarial nature of, 10
Leo, Richard, 4
Lett, Brian, 109–16, 170
lying, conversational strategy of, 27–28, 34, 56–57, 168, 172, 173, 176–77

Macdonald, R. S. B, 139, 156, 157
Mackerley, Alan, 51–57, 169
McCullough, David, 17
McDonald, Kenneth, 18–20
manipulating conversation, 5, 48–49, 97
manipulation of on/off switch. *See also* blocking. xi, 20–21, 49, 94–95, 160–62, 164, 168, 171
manipulative seduction, 32
Manziel, Paul, 89–98, 169
Martino, Joe, 69–80
Miller, Gerald R. and James B. Stiff, 176
misunderstandings, 37
money laundering, 27, 62–63
Mussina, Dr. Joseph, 99–106, 170

new information, 115, 116
Ng, Hung Sik and James J. Bradac, 33
nonlanguage clues, 25, 92–93

O'Barr, William, 33, 36
off-topic response, 43, 115, 178
Ofshe, Richard, 4
on/off signatures. *See also* blocking. 91, 159–60
Orr, Cynthia, 91

pace, 44
Patel, Prakesh, 59–68, 169
persuasion, 26, 31–32
Philips, Susan U., 36
Politeness, 6, 174, 178
Poole, Debra A. and Michael E. Lamb. 29
power
  abuse of, 36
  advantage of, 5–6, 171
  awareness of, 34

claiming, 33
definition of, 31
in conversational strategies, 31–38
inequality of, 183
of police interviewers, 37
of prosecutors, 37
of subordinates, 6
of superordinates, 6, 36
of undercover agents, 36–37
structured, 33
unrecognized, 32–33
unsupervised, 20
pre-close, 154
presence/nonpresence in a conversation, 92–93
presupposition, 15, 161
professional vision, viii, x, 11
prologues and postlogues, 20

questions omitted, 134
questioning tactics, 130–31, 134

recency principle, the, 22, 32, 152, 174
reconstructed dialogue, 127, 133
referencing. 104, 105, 145, 146, 150, 152, 163
reported speech, 132
representations of illegality, 60–63, 146
requesting apologies, 102–06, 170
requesting clarification, 37, 143, 153
requesting directives, 29, 109, 113
requesting scripting, 29
response analysis, 44
retelling, law enforcement undercover step of, 8, 26–27, 51–55, 169, 172
Robinson, W. Peter, 176

Sandoval, Vincent, 9
Scheck, Barry, Peter Neufeld and Jim Dwyer, 7, 131
schema, x, 125, 140
Schiffrin, Deborah, 18, 115
scripting the target, conversational strategy of, 28–29, 34, 37, 52, 55–56, 101, 132, 134, 143, 149, 157, 162, 164, 168, 169, 171, 172, 175

seduction, 32
self-generated guilt, law enforcement undercover step of, 7, 9, 12, 79, 83, 114, 156
Shalash, Tariq, 117–27, 170
shared knowledge, 15, 22, 25, 27
Shuy, Roger W., 4, 7, 16, 18, 23, 25, 26, 28, 176
Silverman, Richard, 26
simultaneous speech, 46–47, 64
Smith, David, 81–88, 169
Solan, Lawrence, 36
Sornig, Karl, 32
speaking for another, 19
speaking on behalf of, 19
speech acts, 7
"speed date," 138
Strickland, Jack, 42, 43, 45
stylistic analysis, 132, 134
Stygall, Gail, 36, 131

tag questions, 115
Tannen, Deborah, 13, 18, 34
tape recording the prologue, 20
Texas Brilab investigation, 28
Tiersma, Peter, 36
Tilsen, Scott, 110
Timing, 45

topic analysis, 6, 43, 44, 46–48, 65, 111, 140, 143, 145, 152, 153, 160, 174–75
Townsend, Jerry, 21, 159–64, 171
trial transcripts, 5, 47–48, 90–96, 126, 127, 132

unabomber (Ted Kaczynski), 181
University of Washington Law School's Innocense Project, 131

Van Dijk, Teun, 35
ventreloquizing, 18
verbal quotes, 72
verbatim recall, 134
voice lowering for covertness, 126, 170

Webb, Robert. 118
Webster, Paul. 69–80
Wenatchee sex ring, 129–36
Werbner, Mark, 82
Williams, Senator Harrison A., 23, 25, 26, 28
withholding crucial information from target, conversational strategy of, 27, 28, 132, 168, 169, 172, 174, 175, 177

Lightning Source UK Ltd.
Milton Keynes UK
UKOW02n2207200415

249970UK00001BA/7/P